MEN & WOMEN
who changed the world

COLLINS

Contributors: Kenneth and Valerie McLeish, Fiona MacDonald
Designers: Susi Martin, Brazzle Atkins, Mike Snell, Paul Reeves
Editors: Susan Dickinson, Sarah Allen
Picture Researchers: Lorraine Sennett, Liz Heasman

© 1997 HarperCollins*Publishers* Ltd
First published in 1997. Reprinted 1999

ISBN 000 198362 8

Printed and Bound by Printing Express Ltd., Hong Kong.

How do you change the world?

Once, people thought that the world was flat. But intrepid sailors and explorers, like Christopher Columbus, proved that it was round, by sailing from east to west and discovering new lands. Other people thought that the Earth was the centre of the Universe and that the Sun and the stars revolved around it. But astronomers, like Copernicus and Galileo, discovered that the Sun was the centre of our solar system and the Earth and the other planets revolved around it.

In this book you will find the stories of these brave people, for even the astronomers were brave, as the Church at that time did not approve of scientists going against the beliefs that had been held for a long time. You will also find stories of rulers, leaders and reformers who changed the way the world was governed by conquering other lands or by transforming and modernizing their own country: people like Alexander the Great, Elizabeth I, Napoleon Bonaparte, Abraham Lincoln, Karl Marx, Indira Gandhi and Nelson Mandela.

There are scientists and inventors – people who invented printing, or who discovered how the telephone worked, or who invented radio and television. There is Charles Darwin, who realized that creatures had been evolving over millions of years and had not, as people thought at the time, remained unchanged since the day of creation. And there are people who made important scientific discoveries in our own century: Marie Curie and her husband Pierre, and Alexander Fleming with the discovery of penicillin.

If it seems that very few women have made important changes to the world, it must be remembered that until quite recently women in many countries had no rights and were regarded as the property of their husband. But women like Elizabeth Cady Stanton, Florence Nightingale, Mary Wollstonecraft, Elizabeth Fry, Margaret Sanger and Emmeline Pankhurst campaigned hard for women's rights. All of them endured mockery, and women were often imprisoned for their beliefs.

Of course, you won't find every single person who over the centuries has made a contribution to the changes in the world. There wouldn't be room in a book of this size. But you will find most of the important ones, with a little bit about what they did and why they are important.

CONTENTS

RULERS & LEADERS

6   Moses

7   Alexander the Great

8   Julius Caesar
    Augustus
    Cleopatra

9   Genghis Khan
    Akbar the Great
    Kublai Khan
    Tamerlane

10 Joan of Arc

11 Elizabeth I

12 Peter the Great
    Catherine the Great

13 Napoleon Bonaparte
    Horatio, Viscount Nelson

14 Abraham Lincoln
    George Washington

15 Winston Churchill
    Adolf Hitler

16 Mao Ze Dong

17 Indira Gandhi
    Sirimavo Bandaranaike
    Benazir Bhutto
    Golda Meir

REFORMERS & CHANGERS

18 Siddhartha Gautama
    (the Buddha)

19 Jesus Christ

20 Muhammad
    Guru Nanak

21 Martin Luther
    John Calvin
    Henry VIII

22 Mary Wollstonecraft
    Elizabeth Fry
    Miranda Stuart

FLORENCE NIGHTINGALE

23 Elizabeth Cady Stanton
    Victoria Woodhull

24 Florence Nightingale
    Mary Seacole
    Mother Teresa

25 Harriet Tubman
    Sojourner Truth

26 Karl Marx
    Vladimir Ilyich Lenin

27 Emmeline Pankhurst
    Emily Davison

28 Maria Montessori
    Friedrich Froebel

29 Margaret Sanger
    Aletta Jacobs
    Marie Stopes

30 Mohandas Karamchand Gandhi

31 Martin Luther King

32 Mikhail Gorbachev
    Vaclav Havel
    Lech Walesa

33 Nelson Mandela
    F.W.de Klerk

SCIENTISTS & INVENTORS

34 **Archimedes**
Hypatia

35 **Johannes Gutenberg**
William Caxton

36 **Galileo Galilei**
Nicolaus Copernicus

37 **Charles Babbage**
Ada Lovelace

38 **Isambard Kingdom Brunel**
George and Robert Stephenson
James Watt

39 **Charles Darwin**

40 **Thomas Edison**
Alexander Graham Bell

41 **Marie and Pierre Curie**

42 **Guglielmo Marconi**
John Logie Baird

43 **Alexander Fleming**
Howard Florey
Louis Pasteur

MEN & WOMEN OF ACTION

44 **Cheng Ho**
James Cook
Marco Polo

45 **Christopher Columbus**
Vasco da Gama

46 **Meriwether Lewis and William Clark**

47 **Simon Bolivar**
Toussaint L'Ouverture

48 **David Livingstone**
Mary Kingsley

49 **Fridtjof Nansen and Roald Amundsen**
Robert Scott

50 **Wilbur and Orville Wright**
Frank Whittle

51 **Yuri Gagarin**
Sally Ride
Valentina Tereshkova

MEN & WOMEN OF ARTS & INDUSTRY

52 **Murasaki Shikibu**
Queen Matilda of Normandy

53 **Leonardo da Vinci**
Michelangelo

54 **William Shakespeare**

55 **Ludwig van Beethoven**
Wolfgang Amadeus Mozart
Clara Schumann

56 **Jane Austen**
Charles Dickens and other writers

57 **Matthew Brady**
Louis Daguerre

58 **Andrew Carnegie**
George Cadbury

59 **Henry Ford**

60 **Claude Monet**
Vincent van Gogh

61 **Pablo Picasso**
Henry Moore

62 **Anna Pavlova**
Sergei Diaghilev
Isadora Duncan

63 **Bill Gates**
Clive Sinclair

YURI GAGARIN

MOSES
HEBREW LEADER c. 13TH CENTURY BC

The story of Moses' life is told in the Bible. Moses' mother was a Hebrew slave in Egypt. At the time of Moses' birth, the pharaoh (Egyptian ruler) had given orders that all new-born Hebrew boys were to be killed. Moses' mother hid her son in a watertight basket among the bulrushes on the River Nile. But when the pharaoh's daughter was bathing in the river she found the baby, and brought Moses up as an Egyptian.

According to the Bible, God told Moses to lead the Hebrews out of slavery in Egypt. But the pharaoh refused to let the Hebrews leave. God sent ten plagues (disasters) to strike Egypt: they included flies, locusts, sickness and death. At last the pharaoh changed his mind and allowed the Hebrews to leave.

As Moses led the Hebrews from Egypt, the pharaoh changed his mind again and sent soldiers after them. It seemed that the Hebrews would be trapped between the Red Sea and their pursuers. But God gave Moses the power to split the Red Sea, and the Hebrews crossed on dry land between walls of water. As the Egyptians tried to follow, the water flowed back, drowning them.

It took 40 years for the Hebrews to cross the desert, but eventually Moses led his people to the promised land of Canaan.

THE BURNING BUSH

THE BURNING BUSH
As a young man, Moses killed an Egyptian who was beating a Hebrew slave. He fled for safety to the desert. There he saw a bush on fire. Flames roared and darted all over the bush, but it remained unharmed. Moses heard God speaking from the bush. God told him to lead the Hebrews out of slavery to a new country called Canaan (later known as Palestine or Israel).

THE TORAH
On their way to Canaan, the Hebrews passed Mount Sinai. God called to Moses and gave him the Torah: the first five books of the Bible containing the Ten Commandments. Jewish people regard Moses as God's lawgiver, and every year at Passover, they celebrate the Exodus – their ancestors' escape from Egypt.

Moses separating the waters of the Red Sea. Illustration from the Luther Bible. (Note that the sea has been painted red.)

ALEXANDER THE GREAT
MACEDONIAN CONQUEROR   356–323 BC

Alexander's father, Philip of Macedonia, was a conqueror. He wanted his son to rule the world. From boyhood, Alexander trained as a soldier and ruler. When he was 20, his father was assassinated and Alexander became king.

Alexander ruled Macedonia (a region now covering part of Greece, Bulgaria and the former Yugoslavia). He conquered Greece and Egypt, but his ambition was to conquer the huge Persian Empire. This stretched for 3,000 kilometres, from the Mediterranean Sea as far as the country we now call Pakistan. It was the richest, most powerful empire in the known world.

It took Alexander only eleven years to conquer the whole Persian Empire. He then planned to follow the River Indus into India, but his soldiers rebelled. They thought that if they went further they would fall prey to giants and flesh-eating monsters. Alexander returned to his palace in Babylon, where he died at the age of 32. The cause of his death is thought to be malaria.

'THE GREATEST'
The Persian army had hundreds of thousands of soldiers. They outnumbered all their enemies. Instead of fighting them head-on, Alexander devised a new method of fighting using a military formation called a phalanx, where the soldiers overlapped their shields, forming a 'wall'. He won battle after battle. His soldiers nicknamed him 'megistos' – 'The Greatest' – and the name has stuck.

Alexander planned to make Asia and Europe one country, with Babylon as its capital. However, after his death Alexander's generals fought among themselves for control of the empire. By 311 BC the empire was split into independent states or monarchies.

KEY DATES
356 BC Born in Pella, Macedonia
336 BC Becomes king of Macedonia
334 BC First victory against the Persians
326 BC Almost invades India, but soldiers mutiny
323 BC Dies, aged 32

JULIUS CAESAR
ROMAN CONSUL
AND GENERAL c.100–44 BC

Caesar believed he was born to rule: he was a politician rather than a soldier, but in 58 BC he began a campaign to conquer Gaul. During this time he overcame the various Gallic tribes, uniting them under Roman rule. On his return to Italy he 'crossed the Rubicon', the stream that marked the boundary between Italy and Gaul. He now faced civil war with the politicians in Rome, but after defeating them, Caesar was supreme in the Roman world. He set about restoring order and prosperity. Conditions in the provinces were improved and Roman citizenship given to non-Romans. He reformed the calendar and had plans for large engineering works. But he had grand ideas of his own importance. He lived in great luxury and had his statue erected in the temple of Romulus. The senators thought he wanted to make himself king and were afraid he would become a tyrant. In 44 BC he made himself dictator for life and on the Ides of March (15th) he was assassinated by a band of conspirators.

AUGUSTUS 63 BC–AD 14
Octavian, later the Emperor Augustus, and great-nephew of Julius Caesar, came to Rome to avenge Caesar's murder and rallied the support of Caesar's old soldiers. With Mark Antony he defeated the army of Caesar's murderers at the Battle of Philippi in 42 BC. Octavian and Antony divided the Roman world between them, but in 31 BC Octavian defeated Antony and Cleopatra at the naval Battle of Actium. Octavian was now supreme in Rome and soon he was given the title 'Augustus'. He consolidated the Roman Empire in the west and built many cities, as well as beautifying Rome itself. At his death, the Empire was strong and established.

ANTONY AND CLEOPATRA
Cleopatra was the last queen of Egypt, immortalized in William Shakespeare's play, *Antony and Cleopatra*. When she and Mark Antony fell in love she persuaded him to leave his wife, Octavia, the sister of Octavian (Emperor Augustus) and set up his 'kingdom' with her in Egypt. Antony had originally worked with Octavian, but after Julius Caesar's death they grew further and further apart and his love for Cleopatra antagonized Octavian. When Antony's army was defeated by Octavian's troops at the Battle of Actium in 31BC, he committed suicide. Devastated by his death, and realizing Egypt was doomed, Cleopatra killed herself by applying an asp, a poisonous snake, to her breast.

KEY DATES

58 BC	Caesar begins Gallic War
49 BC	Caesar crosses Rubicon and faces civil war
44 BC	Appoints himself dictator for life; Caesar murdered
42 BC	Battle of Philippi
31 BC	Battle of Actium
30 BC	Cleopatra commits suicide
AD 14	Augustus dies, aged 77

GENGHIS KHAN
MONGOL RULER c.1162–1227

Genghis Khan was born in Mongolia, a huge country in the centre of Asia. He was called Temujin but was given the name Genghis Khan, a title that probably means 'universal ruler', after becoming ruler of Mongolia. He led his army in successful campaigns against neighbouring countries.

Genghis Khan's soldiers were merciless. When they conquered a town they butchered its people and heaped their skulls by the roadside as a warning to others. At the time of Genghis Khan's death, his empire stretched from the Caspian Sea in the west to the Pacific Ocean in the east.

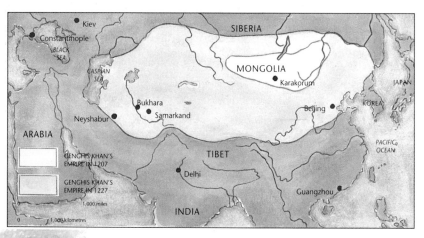

THE MONGOL ARMY

Genghis Khan's army was made up of warriors from scattered nomadic (wandering) tribes, organized into a splendid fighting force. His soldiers were superb horsemen. They attacked with great speed and courage, firing arrows from horseback. Sometimes they would seem to retreat, only to turn suddenly on the confused enemy. Genghis Khan created a corps of Mongols trained in military tactics who were stationed with various tribes as a training force.

KUBLAI KHAN 1216–94

Kublai Khan, Genghis Khan's grandson, conquered China. But once the conquering was done, he ruled fairly and kindly. He built a beautiful capital city, Peking (Beijing). He is well-known to Westerners as a result of Marco Polo's travels.

TAMERLANE (TIMUR) c. 1336–1405

A descendant of Genghis Khan, Tamerlane ascended the throne in Samarkand in 1369 and his soldiers swept south and west into Afghanistan, Persia and India. By the time of his death he was ruler of a vast empire.

AKBAR THE GREAT 1542–1605

Akbar, also a descendant of Genghis Khan, was ruler of the Mughal Empire of north and central India for 49 years. Known for his fairness, he organized a new system of taxation and coinage, and won support from people of all religions.

KEY DATES	
c. 1162	Temujin born
1180	Temujin becomes chief; he starts conquering
1206	Temujin proclaimed Genghis Khan
c. 1216	Kublai Khan born
1227	Genghis Khan dies, aged about 65
1279	Kublai Khan becomes Emperor of China
1294	Kublai Khan dies, aged 78
c. 1336	Tamerlane born
1405	Tamerlane dies, aged about 69
1542	Akbar born
1556	Akbar becomes Mughal Emperor
1605	Akbar dies, aged 63

JOAN OF ARC
FRENCH WARRIOR 1412–31

In 1425, when she was 13, Joan of Arc heard voices, which she believed came from God. They told her to lead the French people against invading English troops. Prince Charles of France gave her soldiers and weapons and in 1429 Joan's army defeated the English. But she was captured by England's allies, put in prison, tried and burnt to death in 1431.

Joan's story is simple and tragic. It is also remarkable because, unlike most women leaders, she did not come from a powerful family. She was a peasant who spent most of her life herding sheep. She had no education and no rich friends. Some people say she was mad; others say she was a saint. She was certainly 'used' to help win a savage war.

BREAKING THE RULES
Joan forced people to listen by breaking the rules about how girls should behave. She was disobedient, demanding and proud (not quiet and gentle). This was dangerous because it made people think she was odd, and it was easy for her political enemies to accuse her of heresy (wrong thinking) and have her burned at the stake.

INSPIRATION
In battle, Joan's courage and determination inspired others. Partly as a disguise and partly for practical reasons in battle, she cut her hair short and wore armour.

KEY DATES	
1412	Joan of Arc born at Domrémy, France
1429	Given soldiers by Prince Charles. Defeats the English at Orleans; Charles is crowned King Charles VII
1431	Tried for heresy and executed (aged only 19) by the English
1920	Made a saint by Catholic Church

QUEEN BOUDICCA (BOADICEA) 1ST CENTURY AD
When Queen Boudicca's husband died during the Roman occupation of Britain, the Roman emperor, Nero, wanted his estate. Boudicca's home was raided and her land seized. Boudicca raised an army to attack the Roman overlords and many thousands of Roman soldiers were killed; but she was finally defeated and took poison on the battlefield, killing herself.

ELIZABETH I 1533–1603
QUEEN OF ENGLAND ruled 1558–1603

Queen Elizabeth I was well-educated, shrewd, cautious and clever. She needed all these qualities: her reign began with unrest at home and threats from abroad. She ruled England for 45 years, negotiating skilfully with politicians, priests and foreign ambassadors. Looking back, some people called it a 'Golden Age'. Trade, exploration, art, music, learning and literature all thrived while she was queen.

Elizabeth saw herself as a symbol of independent England. She wore glorious jewelled clothes to display the nation's wealth. She stayed unmarried for political reasons – if she married, her royal power might pass to a foreign prince.

POWER AT SEA
Elizabeth needed a strong navy to protect England. Her sailors brought the first potatoes and tobacco to England from America. One of these men, Sir Francis Drake, became the first Englishman to sail around the world, from 1577 to 1580.

THE PLAYS OF SHAKESPEARE
The outstanding playwright of Elizabeth's time was William Shakespeare (see page 54). There were several theatres on the south bank of the River Thames, of which the best known is the Globe, where many of Shakespeare's plays were performed.

THE SPANISH ARMADA
Catholic rulers in Europe wanted to end Elizabeth's Protestant reign. In 1588 Philip II of Spain sent a fleet of warships – an 'Armada' – to attack England. The attack failed and, battered by cannons and fierce storms, many Spanish ships sank.

KEY DATES	
1533	Elizabeth born at Greenwich
1536	Elizabeth's father, King Henry VIII, executes her mother, Anne Boleyn
1554	Elizabeth put in prison by her half-sister, Queen Mary I
1558	Mary dies; Elizabeth crowned queen
1603	Elizabeth dies, aged 69

PETER THE GREAT
TSAR OF RUSSIA 1672–1725

Determined to transform and modernize Russia, the Tsar Peter I looked to the West and forcibly introduced Western customs. He improved the army and chose people of ability for high offices, rather than merely handing them to noblemen. After a long war with Sweden, Russian territory was expanded to the Baltic Sea, and a Russian navy was created. In 1712 the city of St Petersburg (see below) on the River Neva was established as the new capital. Peter greatly strengthened the power of the Tsar, increasing his hold over the church, and extending serfdom, but he gave Russia a vigorous start on the road to modernization.

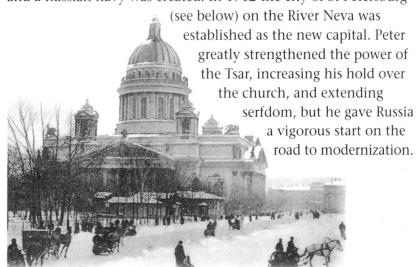

PETER THE GREAT OR PETER THE CRUEL?
For all his gifts and far-sighted visions, Peter was a man of incredible cruelty. As a child he had narrowly escaped death in the murderous feuds between the families of his father's first and second wives. The obstinacy of his subjects often drove him into fits of almost insane rage and he kicked and beat anyone who came in his way. When his subjects disagreed with his reforms for their country, he ruthlessly put down any resistance. At the end of his reign he tortured and killed his only son, Alexis, because he feared Alexis would undo all his hard work after his death.

KEY DATES

1672	Peter born in Moscow
1682	Peter and half-brother Ivan declared joint Tsars, their elder sister Sophia being regent
1689	Peter and Ivan take over administration
1696	Ivan dies; Peter's sole reign begins
1725	Peter the Great dies, aged 53
1729	Catherine born in Prussia
1745	Catherine marries Peter, grandson of Peter the Great, heir to Russian throne
1762	Peter becomes Tsar Peter III; murder of Peter; Catherine declared Empress
1796	Catherine dies, aged 67

CATHERINE THE GREAT – EMPRESS OF RUSSIA 1729–96
Twenty years after Peter's death, a German princess married his grandson, who was a weak, incompetent man. He became Tsar Peter III in 1762, but his wife Catherine quickly took over the responsibilities and soon after Peter III was murdered. Catherine succeeded to the throne and immediately set about expanding what Peter the Great had begun. She improved the education of women, built schools and hospitals, and encouraged scientists, writers and artists from other countries to move to Russia.

  Unfortunately for the majority of the Russian people, the serfs, there was no improvement at all, and any peasant revolts were brutally suppressed. Under Catherine, Russia's frontiers were further extended and she acquired lands along the Black Sea, most of Poland and parts of Siberia.

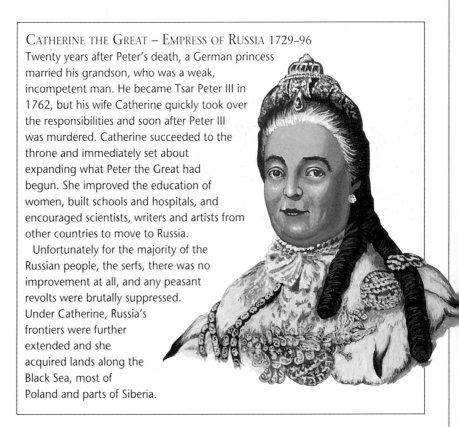

NAPOLEON BONAPARTE
FRENCH SOLDIER AND RULER 1769–1821

As a boy, Napoleon dreamed of equalling the achievements of such generals as Alexander the Great and Julius Caesar, and by the time he was 23, he was an army commander.

In 1799 Napoleon formed a new government in France, and in 1804 he became emperor. At his coronation, he put on his own crown. He said that no priest deserved the honour. He planned to make all Europe one single empire, as in the days of the ancient Roman Empire.

Napoleon was more than just a brilliant soldier. During his time as emperor he reorganized the laws of France. His new system of laws, called the 'Napoleonic Code', is still used in France, as well as in many other countries.

EMPEROR OF EUROPE
Napoleon conquered Italy, Switzerland, Germany and the huge Austrian Empire. Other countries were better at resisting him. The British, Spanish and Portuguese armies pinned his army down for six years in the Peninsular War (1808–14), fought in Portugal and Spain.

KEY DATES

1769	Napoleon born in Corsica
1793	First military successes
1796	Marries Josephine de Beauharnais
1804	Crowned Emperor of France
1805	Defeated by British navy at Battle of Trafalgar
1812	Invades Russia
1815	Defeated at Battle of Waterloo; exiled
1821	Dies, aged 52

END OF A DREAM
Napoleon and his army invaded Russia in 1812 and captured Moscow. His army was victorious and returned to France. On the way home the French soldiers were trapped in the fierce Russian winter, and half a million of them died from disease and frostbite.

Seeing Napoleon's army so weak, the rest of Europe allied together to defeat him. In 1815, at the Battle of Waterloo, Napoleon was beaten by the British and Prussian armies, led by the Duke of Wellington and the Prussian leader Blücher. After his defeat, Napoleon was exiled to the island of St Helena, where he died six years later, in 1821.

HORATIO, VISCOUNT NELSON 1758–1805
Nelson was a brilliant sailor, an inspired leader and a great admiral. Although often obstructive, especially with superiors, he was always generous to those below him. It was Britain's good luck to have such an able man in its navy during the Napoleonic Wars. Never afraid to take risks, Nelson had several outstanding naval victories. Having pursued the French right across the Atlantic and then back again to Spain, Nelson eventually fought both the French and Spanish fleets off Cape Trafalgar in 1805. The Battle of Trafalgar gave Britain naval supremacy for the next 50 years. But Nelson was killed during the battle. Trafalgar Square in London is his memorial.

ABRAHAM LINCOLN
US LAWYER AND PRESIDENT 1809–65

Lincoln's family was poor, and the children had to work instead of going to school. Young Lincoln worked as a labourer, a ferryman on the Ohio River and a clerk. He educated himself from books. At the age of 25, he was a lawyer and soon afterwards he went into politics. In 1860 he was elected president.

SLAVERY AND THE CIVIL WAR

Until the 1860s, there were thousands of slaves in the southern states of the USA. They worked on huge farms called plantations, usually growing cotton. In the northern states, most people felt that slavery was wrong. When Lincoln became president, he passed a law ending slavery. The southern states declared themselves an independent country, separate from the north. Lincoln sent soldiers to the south, and civil war (war between two groups of people from the same country) broke out.

The war lasted for four blood-soaked years, before the southern states surrendered in 1865. Lincoln said that this was the chance to make the country truly the 'United States', to end the bitterness which had caused the war.

'DIE, TYRANT!'

After the Civil War was over, Lincoln still had enemies. On Good Friday, 14th April 1865, he went to the theatre and, in the middle of the play, an actor called John Wilkes Booth pulled out a pistol and shot him dead.

GEORGE WASHINGTON – FIRST PRESIDENT OF THE UNITED STATES 1732–99

George Washington commanded the army that won American independence from Great Britain – an event celebrated every year on 4th July. The United States of Washington's time was very different from today. When he became president there were only eleven states. Five more joined the Union during his presidency, but all the states were east of the Mississippi River and the total population was less than four million. Washington was greatly loved and admired by the American people and the capital, Washington D.C., is named after him.

KEY DATES	
1732	George Washington born
1775	American War of Independence starts
1783	Peace treaty signed
1789	Washington elected first president
1799	Washington dies, aged 67
1809	Abraham Lincoln born
1860	Lincoln elected president
1861	Civil War breaks out
1863	Emancipation of slaves is proclaimed
1865	Civil War ends; Lincoln shot dead, aged 56

WINSTON CHURCHILL
BRITISH PRIME MINISTER 1874-1965

The most famous Englishman of the 20th century, Winston Churchill first entered Parliament in 1900 at the age of 26. In 1911 he was made First Lord of the Admiralty and devoted much energy into equipping and preparing the Navy should war occur. After the First World War Churchill held various government posts, and frequently warned the House of the dangers of the increasing power of Hitler in Germany. But his warnings were not heeded and he was called a warmonger.

At the beginning of the Second World War the Germans and their allies, the Italians, had soon overrun nearly the whole of Europe. In 1940 when it seemed that a German invasion of Great Britain was imminent, Churchill became British Prime Minister. As a result of his leadership, courage and the power of his broadcasts to the British people, Great Britain held firm against Hitler's aggression. After Russia and the USA entered the war in 1941 the tide began to turn. Victory for the free world was proclaimed in 1945.

After the war, Churchill was Prime Minister again in 1951 for a period of four years. When he died in 1965 he was awarded a state funeral.

THE BATTLE OF BRITAIN
In May 1940 the British people were expecting Germany to invade. But German forces could not cross the Channel until they had first destroyed the Royal Air Force. In August 1940 the German air force began daylight raids on England in an attempt to destroy British air power. But the RAF fought back bravely, aided by a new invention – radar. By October the immediate danger of invasion had passed, and the Germans were concentrating instead on night bombing raids on British cities.

ADOLF HITLER 1889-1945
After World War I, millions of Germans were without jobs, and German money had lost its value. Hitler, an ex-soldier, was determined to put the country back on its feet. He became leader of the Nationalist Socialist (Nazi) Party, and in 1933 Chancellor of Germany, ruling as dictator. He rebuilt the German army, navy and air force, and in 1938 invaded Austria and Czechoslovakia. In 1939 Hitler's attack on Poland triggered the Second World War, during which the Nazis terrorized Europe and murdered 6 million Jews. Shortly before Germany's defeat in 1945, Hitler committed suicide.

KEY DATES

1900	Churchill enters Parliament
1911	First Lord of the Admiralty
1940	Made Prime Minister
1945	End of World War II
1951	Prime Minister for second time
1965	Dies in London

MAO ZE DONG (MAO TSE TUNG)
CHINESE LEADER 1893–1976

Mao's father was a farmer, and Mao grew up in the countryside. He saw that farm labourers were often overworked, hungry and poor. Only those people who owned the land had an easy life. Mao decided that communism was the answer: all the land would belong to the state, and everyone would work and be treated the same.

THE 'LONG MARCH'
When Chiang Kai Shek became leader of the Nationalist party in 1925, war between the Nationalists and Communists soon developed. Chiang tried to exterminate the Communists from their province in southern China. In 1934 Mao set out with nearly 100,000 followers, men, women and children, on the 'Long March', (9,700 km) to safety. The terrible hardships they endured on this year-long trek welded the Communists into a tightly-knit force.

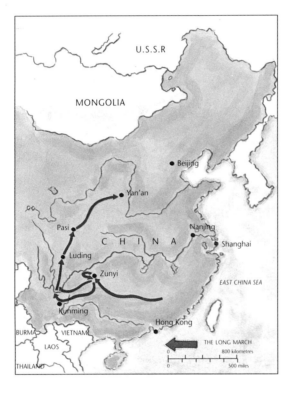

PEACE AND WAR
In 1937 Japan, an ally of Germany, attacked China. All of China joined to fight the aggressors. But after the war, in 1945, the two sides in China split again. Chiang's supporters were driven out of China and went to live on the island of Taiwan. Mao's followers stayed in China, and made it a communist state.

MAOISM
In 1949 Mao was Chairman of the Chinese Communist Party. He held on to power by suppressing any opposition and severely punishing anyone who criticized him. In 1958 he launched the Great Leap Forward with unreachable targets for industrial production As a result, about 20 million people died of starvation.

THE LITTLE RED BOOK
Mao's peasant beginnings made him distrustful of educated people, and doctors and teachers were forced to work on the land. Everyone had to carry with them at all times the Little Red Book, which contained the thoughts and sayings of Chairman Mao.

KEY DATES	
1893	Born in Shaoshan, Hunan Province, China
1918	Begins work in a Beijing library
1921	Helps found the Chinese Communist Party
1934	The 'Long March'
1939-45	Second World War
1949	Chinese Revolution; Mao becomes Chairman of the People's Republic of China
1976	Dies, aged 83

INDIRA GANDHI
INDIAN PRIME MINISTER 1917–84

Indira Gandhi, first woman Prime Minister of India, was a member of a powerful political family. Her father, Jawaharlal Nehru, had been Prime Minister, and her son, Rajiv, would be Prime Minister after his mother.

From her earliest years, Gandhi was trained for a political career. As a child, she met international leaders who visited her home. With her father, she joined in the struggle to win freedom from British control. Later, she helped him rule.

As Prime Minister, Indira Gandhi attracted both praise and blame. She worked to improve living conditions and to encourage farming and industry. She made India respected abroad. But she treated those who disagreed with her harshly. At times, it seemed as if her actions might lead to civil war. She was eventually murdered by her own Sikh bodyguards.

THE GOLDEN TEMPLE

The Golden Temple at Amritsar in India is a holy place for members of the Sikh faith. Only Sikhs are allowed to enter. In 1984 there were clashes between Sikhs wanting a separate homeland and the Indian government. Sikh leaders took refuge in the Temple. Gandhi ordered soldiers who were not Sikhs to go into the Temple and capture them. In the fighting that followed, over 400 people were killed.

GOLDA MEIR – PRIME MINISTER OF ISRAEL 1898–1978

Born Golda Mabovitz in Kiev, in the Ukraine, her family went to Milwaukee, Wisconsin, USA in 1906 and Golda later became a school teacher. In 1921 she went to Palestine, which in 1948 was divided into the new nation of Israel and Arab states. She held various posts in the Israeli government and in 1969 Golda Meir became Prime Minister of Israel. She maintained a firm but fair policy towards the Arabs, but throughout her ministry there was conflict between the Israelis and the Arabs. In 1973 war broke out for the fourth time. She was criticized for Israel's early losses and resigned the premiership in 1974.

SIRIMAVO BANDARANAIKE – SRI LANKAN POLITICIAN BORN 1916

Mrs Bandaranaike the world's first woman Prime Minister dominated Sri Lankan politics of 17 years. She was made president of the Sri Lanka Freedom Party in 1960 and was Prime Minister , from 1960 to 1965 and from 1970 to 1977.

BENAZIR BHUTTO – PAKISTANI POLITICIAN BORN 1953

Benazir Bhutto, the daughter of Zulfikar Ali Bhutto who was murdered in 1979, became the leader of the Pakistan People's Party in 1984, becoming the first female Muslim Prime Minister in 1988. She was at loggerheads with her generals over her policies and was removed by presidential decree in 1990, accused of corruption. Re-elected in 1993, she was again removed in 1996.

BENAZIR BHUTTO

KEY DATES	
1917	Indira Gandhi born in Allahabad, India
1947–64	Works with her father while he is Prime Minister of India
1966	First woman Prime Minister of India
1975	Criticized for abusing power
1984	Murdered by Sikh bodyguards

17

SIDDHARTHA GAUTAMA
THE BUDDHA – FOUNDER OF BUDDHISM
C. 563–483 BC

According to tradition, Siddhartha Gautama was born the son of a king in the foothills of the Himalayas. At the age of 29, greatly troubled by the unsolved mystery of old age, sickness and death, but inspired by the sight of a wandering holy man, he felt impelled to leave everything in search of an answer. After six years of heroic effort, during which he almost died, he finally discovered the answer he sought. From this time on he became known as 'the Buddha' (the Awakened One). For the rest of his life, until his death at the age of 80, the Buddha taught how suffering comes to be, how it can be ended, and the way or path to wisdom. This path is known as the Noble Eightfold Path, because it contains eight steps to wisdom.

The Buddha is neither a god nor a prophet, but a great teacher.

THE DALAI LAMA

In the 7th century AD monks from India introduced Buddhism into Tibet, where it combined with traditional Tibetan religious beliefs. The Buddhist leader of the Tibetan people is known as the Dalai Lama. By tradition, he is believed to be the embodiment of Awakening or Enlightenment. When a Dalai Lama dies, his spirit is believed to enter the body of a baby boy who has been born at about the time of his death. Lamas search the country for the right boy, who, when discovered, becomes the next Dalai Lama. For hundreds of years the Dalai Lama was the supreme ruler in Tibet, but after the Chinese invaded the country in 1950, the Dalai Lama was eventually forced to flee to India, where he remains in exile.

BUDDHISM

Those who follow the teachings of Buddha are called Buddhists. Today, there are over 300 million followers worldwide, mainly in the East but also in the West.

The faith of all Buddhists is centred on the Buddha, his teachings (the Dharma) and the religious community (the Sangha) he founded.

KEY POINTS

The Buddha lived in northern India in the 5th and 6th centuries BC

'Buddha' means the 'Enlightened One' or the 'Awakened One'

The Buddha was a great teacher

Buddhism is a way of life leading to wisdom and the end of suffering and unhappiness

JESUS CHRIST
RELIGIOUS LEADER c. 4 BC–c. AD 30

Jesus has been given the title 'Christ', from the Greek word *christos*, meaning 'the anointed one'.

Jesus was born to Mary and Joseph, a carpenter, and brought up in Nazareth in what we now call Israel. Almost nothing is known of his early life, but when he was about 30 he started to teach the people about God's love for each one of them, however humble. He chose twelve followers, his disciples, who were to help him in his teachings. Together they travelled through the land we now call Israel, where Jesus preached to thousands about the love of God, the importance of compassion and forgiveness, and that the way to God is through prayer. He was far ahead of the thoughts and opinions of his own time and he wanted people to think of God as a loving God, not as a God to be feared.

THE RESURRECTION
When Jesus went to Jerusalem for the Jewish Passover festival he was hailed by the crowds in the streets as the King of the Jews and they strewed palm leaves before him. But the Jewish High Priests ordered him to be arrested and he was condemned to death for claiming to be the son of God – a sin. He was nailed to a cross (the usual method of executing people in Roman times) and left to die. On the Sunday following his death on the cross, Jesus' friend Mary Magdalene went to his tomb. She found the stone in front of the tomb had been rolled away and the tomb empty. Soon after this Jesus appeared to Mary Magdalene and the disciples and to a few others. This return to life is known as the Resurrection and is celebrated by Christians every year at Easter.

CHRISTIANITY
The life and death of Jesus are the basis of the Christian religion, whose followers believe that he was the son of God, and that there is life after death. The name 'Christian' was not used until about ten years after Jesus' death. The teachings of Jesus and the accounts of his life are found in the Bible. There are more than a billion Christians in the world.

THE TEACHINGS OF JESUS
Jesus taught in a number of ways, some of them very remarkable. Sometimes he taught through parables, which are stories that illustrated the point he was making. He also taught through miracles when he did seemingly impossible things, for example, when five thousand people were fed from five loaves and two fishes. Usually he taught by preaching on the lakeside or on the side of a hill where large numbers of people could hear him.

KEY POINTS
Born in Bethlehem
Starts teaching about age 30
Tried and crucified in Jerusalem about age 33
Taught that he was the son of God and that there is life after death

MUHAMMAD (MOHAMMED)
RELIGIOUS LEADER   c. 570–632

About 1,400 years ago, Makkah (Mecca) was one of the richest towns in Arabia. It was an important centre for trade and culture. There were places of worship to many gods, and thousands of pilgrims visited the city every year.

Muhammad lived in Mecca. His belief was that there was only one God, not many, and he was God's messenger. His task was to tell of living a simple, holy life, obeying God. He taught about this way of life:

Islam ('submission'). Soon there were many followers of Islam (Muslims). With rising hostility among the leaders of Mecca, Muhammad decided to move to Medina where he knew he would be welcomed. The Muslim calendar dates from the year of Muhammad's migration from Mecca to Medina.

ISLAMIC ART
Islamic artists were forbidden to show the faces of Muhammad or his family because it was seen as trespassing on God's position as sole creator of life. Hence in this picture, which depicts Muhammad pledging his daughter to her suitor, the faces are not shown.

THE QUR'AN (KORAN)
This is the holy book of Islam, and Muslims believe that it contains God's own words, told to Muhammad through the angel Gabriel. This is why they call Muhammad 'God's messenger'. The teaching of the Koran is that there is only one God. Daily prayers are required and brotherly love is stressed. Muslims believe Muhammad was the last of the prophets sent by God. Jesus and certain prophets of the Old Testament came before him.

KEY DATES	
c. 570	Muhammed born at Mecca, now in Saudi Arabia
c. 610	Begins preaching and teaching
622	Migrates to Medina
630	Returns to Mecca
632	Dies, aged about 62

GURU NANAK 1469–1539
This Indian religious leader founded the religion of Sikhism, which combines Islamic and Hindu ideas. Nanak was born a Hindu, at Talwandi in modern-day Pakistan. As a boy he trained to be an accountant, like his father, but his thoughts constantly turned to God. Nanak lived in an area that was deeply divided between Muslims and Hindus, but he believed that God was more important than religious differences. Nanak taught that if people try to love God and do what He wants, then God will teach them to be better people. Nanak was a guru – a religious teacher who led people to the light. On his death, aged 70, he was succeeded by Guru Angad (1539–1552), who collected Nanak's hymns and developed the script for writing them down.

MARTIN LUTHER
LEADER OF THE REFORMATION   1483–1546

Before the Reformation, religion in Europe was held together entirely by the Catholic Church. But the Church had been abusing its power: spending money lavishly on palaces for the clergy, even selling important positions in the Church. The power of the kings in western Europe increased and some of them broke away from the Pope, the head of the Catholic Church.

In 1517 Martin Luther, a Catholic priest in Germany, dared to criticize what he believed to be abuses within the Church. He declared that people could only be saved by faith in Jesus Christ. He also denounced the selling of pardons to sinners. In 1521 the Pope excommunicated him (he was not allowed to take communion or to say prayers with other Catholics) and he was outlawed. But certain German princes supported him and protested against the decisions made against Luther. (The word 'protestant' means 'protester'.) Luther is also famous for his translation of the Bible into German.

RESULTS

The result of the Reformation in Europe was to create a division between the Catholic countries in the south and the Protestant countries in the north. Many different Protestant denominations developed. The Protestants stressed family life, hard work, and the careful spending of money. They also encouraged reading and education. Teachers were people of great importance.

KEY DATES	
1517	Luther protests against church practices
1572	St Bartholemew's Day Massacre
1598	Edict of Nantes gives Huguenots permission to worship
1534	Act of Supremacy in England
1611	Authorized Version of the Bible published

HENRY VIII 1491–1547
In England Henry VIII used the Reformation to please his own desires. The Pope refused to cancel Henry's first marriage with the Spanish princess, Catherine of Aragon, when the king wanted to marry Anne Boleyn, in the hope of getting a son and heir. In 1534 the English parliament passed the Act of Supremacy, making the king the head of the Church in England, thus allowing Henry to marry Anne Boleyn, although at heart Henry remained a Catholic.

JOHN CALVIN 1509–64
Another Protestant, John Calvin, worked out a form of church government whereby a group of 'elders' managed each church. Calvin's followers in France were called Huguenots (hew-gen-ohs) and the Catholic kings in France tried to prevent them from becoming established. On 24th August 1572 (St Bartholomew's Day) thousands of Huguenots in Paris and other French towns were murdered by Catholic supporters. This is now known as the St Bartholomew's Day Massacre.

MARY WOLLSTONECRAFT 1759–97
ENGLISH CAMPAIGNER FOR WOMEN'S RIGHTS

Mary Wollstonecraft lived in exciting times. In many parts of the world, people were fighting to change society. In France, in 1789, politicians published a *Declaration of the Rights of Man*, as part of their plans for a revolution. Mary Wollstonecraft felt that women's rights should be considered too. She studied politics and current affairs. In 1792 she wrote a book demanding equal rights for women. She called for better education, fair treatment in marriage, the right to own property and to control your own life. People were shocked at these bold new ideas. One (male) writer called her 'a hyena in petticoats'.

ELIZABETH FRY 1780–1845

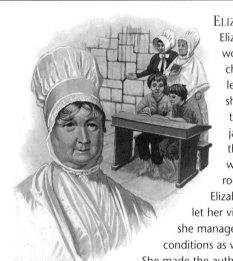

Elizabeth Fry was a serious young woman and, despite having 11 children, found time to help those less well off than herself. When she was 33 a friend told her about the women prisoners in Newgate jail. Many of the prisoners had their children with them and they were all locked up in one filthy room holding 300 people.

Elizabeth Fry persuaded the jailers to let her visit the prisoners and gradually she managed to obtain much better conditions as well as schooling for the children. She made the authorities realize that if prisoners are treated better, they will behave better.

THE FIRST FEMALE DOCTOR IN BRITAIN

When Miranda Stuart (1795–1865) was young, women were not permitted to be lawyers, doctors or priests. But she was determined, and in order to enter Edinburgh's famous medical school she cut her hair short, wore men's clothes and changed her name to James Barry. 'James Barry' passed all her exams and became an army doctor. She worked in the Crimea at the same time as Florence Nightingale, who never suspected that Dr Barry was a woman.

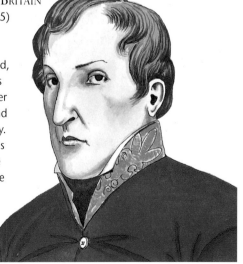

MARRIAGE

In Mary Wollstonecraft's time, a woman gave up all civil rights when she married. She became her husband's property. Even her clothes belonged to him. Wollstonecraft felt that marriage should not be like this; a husband and wife should be equal. Her husband, the philosopher William Godwin, agreed. It wasn't until nearly 100 years after her death that married women were allowed to own property and manage their own income.

KEY DATES

1759	Mary Wollstonecroft born in London, England
1783	Opens a school offering equal education to boys and girls
1792	Visits France to study the Revolution; writes *Vindication of the Rights of Woman*
1797	Dies in childbirth, aged 38

OTHER WOMEN CAMPAIGNERS

Born in 1921, the American author Betty Friedan became famous with the publication of her book, *The Feminine Mystique* (1963). In this, she claimed that society put pressure on women not to seek a career. She is regarded as the founder of the women's liberation movement in the United States. Other important authors who have campaigned for women's rights are: Simone de Beauvoir (French, 1908–86), Nawal El Saadawi (Egyptian, born 1931) and Germaine Greer (Australian, born 1939).

ELIZABETH CADY STANTON 1815–1902
US CAMPAIGNER FOR WOMEN'S RIGHTS

Elizabeth Cady was a disappointment to her father because she was not a boy, but she was determined to prove that girls could do well. She studied law, especially the law concerning women, and was appalled at the unequal treatment women received. Even though she married young and had seven children, she decided to devote her life (and her tremendous energy) to women's rights. In 1869 she founded a campaign to win votes for women. She worked with Amelia Bloomer (1818–94) and Susan B. Anthony (1820–1906) to write a history of the women's movement. She published a newspaper (*The Lily*) and gave lectures.

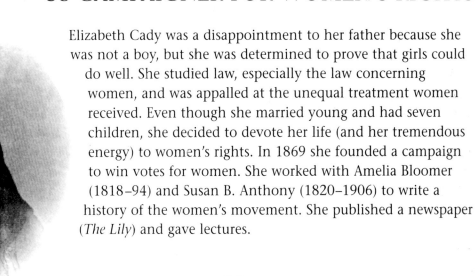

WOMEN NOT ALLOWED

Elizabeth Cady's husband, Henry Stanton, was also interested in social reform. On honeymoon, they travelled to London to attend a conference against slave trading. Only men were allowed to enter the hall. Cady was outraged. Back in the USA, she organized the first Women's Rights Convention and spoke out boldly for property rights for married women. After the Civil War, when voting rights were given to black men, she demanded that women should also have the vote. She continued her campaigns after her husband's death, and also demanded equality for women in the Church.

'BLOOMERS'

Feminist campaigners believed their lives would be improved if they wore comfortable clothes that let them move freely. 'Rational dress' – a short frock over baggy trousers – was invented for gardening in 1851 by Elizabeth Miller (Cady Stanton's niece). These trousers soon became known as 'bloomers' after Amelia Bloomer, one of the first women to wear them. At first, women in trousers were insulted, but after bicycles became popular in the 1890s, trousers for women were accepted as they were more practical.

KEY DATES	
1815	Elizabeth Cady Stanton born in Johnstown, USA
1848	Organizes first Women's Rights Convention at Seneca Falls, USA
1850	Meets Susan B. Anthony
1869	Begins campaign to win votes for American women
1898	Publishes inspiring life-story, *Eighty Years and More*
1902	Dies, aged 87
1920	American women allowed to vote

VICTORIA WOODHULL 1838–1927

Victoria Woodhull was one of the first women bankers in the USA. She worked for women's rights in America and in Britain. In 1872 she was the first ever woman candidate in the US presidential elections. She was unsuccessful, but she showed that women could have ambitions and should aim high.

FLORENCE NIGHTINGALE
ENGLISH NURSING PIONEER 1820–1910

When Florence Nightingale began work, nurses were not trained. They were often rough and careless, and sometimes drunk. Hospitals were so badly run that sick people were more likely to get well again if they were cared for at home. Florence Nightingale hoped to do something useful with her life, but her parents wanted her to marry. At last, aged 30, she got permission to leave home. In 1854 she led a group of 38 women who had volunteered to nurse British soldiers injured in Russia, where the British army was fighting in the Crimean War. Conditions were horrific – dirt and disease killed many more men than injuries in battle – but Nightingale was tough. She insisted on clean, well-run wards and on high standards of nursing. Her achievements won great admiration. For the rest of her life, she worked to improve training for nurses and hospital care.

KEY DATES	
1820	Florence Nightingale born in Florence, Italy
1851	Visits Germany to study nursing
1853	Superintendent in a London hospital
1854	Works in the Crimea, Russia
1860	Founds training school for nurses
1910	Dies, aged 90

MARY SEACOLE 1805 – 81
Mary Seacole was a black nurse who left home in Jamaica and travelled to Russia to help in the Crimean war where she worked with Florence Nightingale. After being awarded medals for bravery she went on to found hospitals in London, the USA and the Caribbean.

'WOMEN'S WORK'

Nursing was usually hard and dirty work. In the hospitals in the Crimea, rats ran between the beds. There were no lavatories, only buckets. Yet, for some women nursing provided an escape from narrow, house-bound lives. Slowly, men came to approve of women doing jobs needing patience and gentleness. It fitted in with their idea of women as 'angels', who devoted their lives to caring for others. It was also convenient: in 1909, one feminist writer described 'women's work' as 'the jobs men don't want to do'.

Nightingale became a heroine. She was known as 'the Lady with the Lamp', because she made a habit of visiting each ward at night-time. Songs and poems praised her work. This sweet, sentimental image was not true: she was brisk and businesslike, and criticized many women for idle, wasted lives.

MOTHER TERESA 1910-1997
After working in a nunnery in India for nearly twenty years, Mother Teresa decided to go to live and work in the Calcutta slums.

She opened her first school in December 1948, and by 1968 had set up health centres in Venezuela, Sri Lanka, and Tanzania. Mother Teresa received the Nobel Peace Prize in 1979.

HARRIET TUBMAN
US FREEDOM FIGHTER FOR AMERICAN SLAVES   1821–1913

Harriet Tubman was born a slave in the southern USA, where slavery was widespread. In 1849, she ran away from her master and vowed to return to help others to escape. Although it was a crime to help a runaway slave, Tubman led hundreds of slaves to freedom via the 'Underground Railroad'. During the Civil War, Tubman used her local knowledge to help northern armies and worked as a scout, a nurse and a spy. After the war she helped raise money for black schools.

A SLAVE'S LIFE
Slaves were bought and sold like cattle and 'belonged' to their master. Husbands and wives could be sold separately and it was a crime to try to escape.

KEY DATES	
1821	Harriet Tubman born in Maryland, USA
1849	Runs away to freedom
1851	Begins working for the 'Underground Railroad', helping slaves to escape
1857	Helps her family to escape
1861	Helps northern troops in Civil War
1865	Civil War ends; slavery abolished
1913	Dies, aged 92

THE 'UNDERGROUND RAILROAD'
This was not a track for trains, but a 'line' of hiding places in cellars, sheds and barns. They were used by runaway slaves as shelters on the dangerous journey from their owners' homes to freedom in the northern USA. Some people gave the runaways food and clothing. Harriet Tubman helped to run the 'railroad'. She was so successful that slave-owners offered a reward of $40,000 to anyone who could catch her.

SOJOURNER TRUTH 1797–1883
Sojourner Truth was born a slave. She won her freedom, and spent the rest of her life as a wandering Christian preacher. She campaigned for equal rights for black people and for every woman's right to vote.

KARL MARX
GERMAN THINKER 1818–83

Marx studied philosophy at university, and then worked as a journalist. He wrote about economics (the way countries make and manage money). His ideas were new, and many people disliked them. There were riots when he appeared in public. He moved from country to country, and finally settled in London.

Marx said that there were two main ways for modern countries to run their economic affairs. The first was capitalism. In this, people with money (capital) used it to buy materials, factories and workers. Capitalism gave unfair power to one group of people (the capitalists), and barred it from another (the workers). In *Das Kapital,* Marx's major work, he discussed what he saw as the strengths and faults of capitalism.

The second way was communism. In this, everyone shared the work to be done, owned part of everything in the state, and took a share of all profits. Marx said that this second stage could only be reached by a 'class struggle', when workers revolted against the power of their bosses.

MARXISM

Marx's ideas ('Marxism') horrified people in power. None of them wanted to lose their money, influence, perhaps even their lives, in a 'class struggle'. But his ideas gave hope to millions who lived in poverty. In the 20th century, there were Marxist revolutions in many countries, especially Russia and China. At one point, over half the world was communist.

Karl Marx is buried in Highgate cemetery in north London, where his grave is marked by an impressive monument.

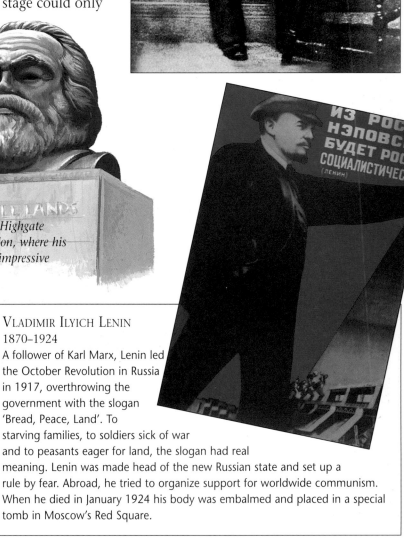

KEY DATES	
1818	Karl Marx born in Trier, Prussia (now Germany)
1843	Marries his childhood sweetheart, Jenny
1848	Writes the *Communist Manifesto* with Friedrich Engels
1849	Settles in London
1867	Writes *Das Kapital,* setting out his ideas on capitalism
1883	Dies, aged 64

VLADIMIR ILYICH LENIN
1870–1924
A follower of Karl Marx, Lenin led the October Revolution in Russia in 1917, overthrowing the government with the slogan 'Bread, Peace, Land'. To starving families, to soldiers sick of war and to peasants eager for land, the slogan had real meaning. Lenin was made head of the new Russian state and set up a rule by fear. Abroad, he tried to organize support for worldwide communism. When he died in January 1924 his body was embalmed and placed in a special tomb in Moscow's Red Square.

EMMELINE PANKHURST
ENGLISH POLITICAL REFORMER   1858–1928

Emmeline Pankhurst was one of the leaders of the Women's Social and Political Union, often called the 'suffragettes'. Together with many brave colleagues, she campaigned for women's right to vote. This was not a new demand. Women had been holding meetings and organizing petitions for over 40 years, but men had ignored them. The suffragettes decided it was time to fight. They would force men to listen. So they smashed shop windows, disrupted elections and wrote 'Votes for Women' all over public buildings. When they were arrested and sent to prison, they argued their case in court. In 1918 the British Parliament gave votes to women over 30. This was partly due to the suffragettes, but men had also seen how women could work for their country during the First World War.

ARREST

The suffragettes feared that their campaign would fail without publicity. So they deliberately broke the law to get arrested. They knew the newspapers would report their trials. They took great care not to hurt people, just to damage property, but they were attacked by angry mobs on many occasions.

When arrested, suffragettes were often roughly handled by the police. When they were sent to prison, if they refused to eat, they were brutally force-fed with tubes through the nose. Today this would be classed as torture. Yet despite their terrible experiences in prison, when they were released and had recovered from their ordeal, they often got themselves re-arrested.

EMILY DAVISON 1872–1913

In 1913 crowds gathered to watch the Derby – a famous horse race. As the king's horse ran past, Emily Davison rushed out, and threw herself under its hooves. She was horribly injured, and died a few days later. A paper with 'Votes for Women' was found pinned to her clothes. Davison had already suffered greatly for her beliefs – she had been force-fed 49 times in prison.

KEY DATES	
1858	Emmeline Pankhurst born in Manchester, England
1879	Marries lawyer, Richard Pankhurst
1903	Founds Women's Social and Political Union
1908	Decides on 'direct action'
1918	Joins Conservative Party; starts new campaign for child welfare; women over 30 win the vote
1928	Dies, aged 70; all women in Britain win the vote

MARIA MONTESSORI
ITALIAN EDUCATIONAL REFORMER   1870–1952

Today, in infant schools, many young children 'learn through play'. They have brightly coloured toys; their paintings are pinned to the walls; teachers encourage them to discover things for themselves. A hundred years ago, schools were very different. Pupils sat at uncomfortable desks, arranged in rigid rows; lessons consisted of learning things by heart; if children made mistakes, they were beaten. This revolution in schooling was inspired mainly by Maria Montessori, an Italian doctor. She worked with children who had problems of many kinds. Although people criticized her ideas, she showed that with kindness and understanding, these children could learn. Montessori was convinced that all children learned better when they were happy and interested, rather than frightened or bored. She worked hard to spread her 'Montessori Method' all round the world.

'PROBLEM' CHILDREN
At first, people did not believe Montessori's teaching methods would work. In 1907 she took charge of a crèche, the Casa dei Bambini, in a slum district of Rome. She took pupils whom no one else would educate. Most were poor, many were neglected. She taught them to read and write, to calculate, to paint, to dance and to sing in a spontaneous way with no prizes or punishments. Her 'backward' children entered for exams with superb results.

KEY DATES	
1870	Maria Montessori born near Ancona, Italy
1894	Qualifies as a doctor
1907	Opens a school in Rome
1922	Made Inspector of Schools for Italy; writes and lectures on education
1952	Dies, aged 82

FRIEDRICH FROEBEL 1782–1852
Froebel opened his first 'kindergarten', or 'garden for children', in Germany in 1837. He believed children should be allowed to grow and develop naturally like plants, and was the first to realize that children learn best when they are happy. To Froebel, free play and games were an important part of learning. By 1900 there were kindergartens in leading cities all over the world.

MARGARET SANGER
US BIRTH-CONTROL PIONEER   1883–1966

While working as a nurse, Margaret Sanger cared for women who were ill after having children, or after having dangerous, illegal abortions. Many of these women died. Others were too weak to look after the children they already had. Yet they went on having babies. Why was this? Many women did not know how to limit their families – birth-control education was banned. Some husbands demanded many children – it was their legal right. The main problem was money. Birth-control supplies were simply too expensive for ordinary people to afford. Sanger gave talks to young mothers about ways of birth control. She was arrested, but that did not stop her. Her pioneering work improved many families' lives.

CLINICS FOR WOMEN
Margaret Sanger knew that many women preferred to be treated by women doctors and nurses. In 1916 she opened a women's clinic in New York run by well-qualified female staff. But the authorities closed it down and Sanger was sentenced to 30 days in the workhouse for causing a 'public nuisance'. Today, clinics like this are common; Sanger's idea has been copied all round the world.

WOMEN'S HEALTH
Aletta Jacobs (1851–1929) was the first recognized woman doctor in Holland. She was particularly concerned with the poor, and ran a free surgery for them, including courses on child care. In 1882 she opened the world's first birth-control clinic in Amsterdam. She was also an active suffragist and in 1894 started the Association for Women's Suffrage. Women in Holland achieved the vote in 1919.

KEY DATES

1883	Margaret Sanger born in Corning, USA
1912	Begins working as a nurse
1914	Publishes magazine, *Woman Rebel*
1916	Flees to Europe, meets Marie Stopes and Aletta Jacobs
1927	Organizes first World Population Conference
1966	Dies, aged 83

SEX EDUCATION
Marie Stopes (1880–1958), a Scot brought up in England, was the first woman to join the Science Faculty at Manchester University in 1904. In 1916 she pioneered a crusade to make women better informed on birth control and sex education, and in 1921 opened a birth-control clinic in London. A public health doctor accused her of a 'monstrous crime' in giving the public information about contraception.

MOHANDAS KARAMCHAND GANDHI
INDIAN POLITICIAN   1869–1948

Gandhi trained to be a lawyer, and then went to South Africa. He worked there for 21 years, fighting laws that treated Indians differently from white people. Gandhi wanted people of different nationality, religion and colour to understand each other. In his own country, India, Hindus divided people into four groups called castes, and members of each caste could have nothing to do with people of a lower caste. When Gandhi returned from South Africa, he worked to remove such barriers.

Gandhi himself was born into the Hindu merchant caste, but he was very concerned at the way people with no caste were 'untouchable'. He campaigned to improve their position, and instead of calling them 'outcastes' he used the name 'harijans' – children of God. Soon Gandhi was also working to free India from British rule. He told people not to use violence to get their way. Instead, they should refuse to co-operate. In about 1920 Gandhi began a programme of hand-spinning and weaving, which he believed would help India in its fight for independence by making it self-sufficient. During the Second World War, Gandhi continued his struggle for India's independence through non-violent disobedience to British rule. India was granted independence in 1947.

FREEDOM AND DEATH
With freedom from British rule, India was divided into two nations: India for the Hindus and Pakistan for the Muslims. As a Hindu, Gandhi was greatly saddened by the rioting between the two groups. He wanted people to live in harmony, but he was murdered by a Hindu who opposed this idea. His death was mourned by millions.

KEY DATES	
1869	Ghandi born in Porbandar, India
1893	Travels to South Africa to work
1915	Returns to India
1915	Given the name 'Mahatma' ('Great Soul')
1919	Begins work for Indian independence
1947	India wins independence
1948	Shot dead, aged 78

MARTIN LUTHER KING
US CIVIL RIGHTS LEADER 1929–68

Martin Luther King studied to be a church pastor (minister) like his father, and in 1954 began work in that role in the town of Montgomery, the state capital of Alabama.

One day King and his father went into a shop to buy shoes. The shopkeeper refused to serve them, because they were sitting in seats reserved for white people. That was when King decided to work for equal rights for all Americans, whatever their skin colour. He told his supporters to follow Gandhi's example in India, and use non-violence to win their way.

King and his followers slowly but surely won the battle for equal rights. In 1964 the government passed a law stating that all Americans should be treated equally. Only a year later white officials in Alabama tried to deny black citizens the right to vote. A march to Montgomery was broken up by the police, using tear gas and clubs. This bloody attack was seen by millions on television, and a few months later the Voting Rights Act of 1965 was passed. Martin Luther King was assassinated in Memphis, Tennessee in April 1968. .

NON-VIOLENT PROTEST

King carried out a policy of protest by non-violence. This was often successful. For example, thousands of black people refused to use the buses in the city of Montgomery after a black woman was arrested for sitting on a 'white' seat. After a year the company changed its seating policy. In 1963 King led a huge march in Washington D.C. This was another way of protesting non-violently.

KEY DATES	
1929	King born in Atlanta, USA
1954	Becomes pastor in Montgomery, Alabama
1955	Begins work for equal rights
1964	Civil Rights Act passed; King wins Nobel Peace Prize
1968	Assassinated, aged 39

BLACK AMERICANS

Although slavery ended in 1865, many black Americans still lived in terrible conditions 90 years later. They had poor housing and education, and in some states they were not allowed to vote. In many towns, black Americans were not allowed to attend the same schools as white Americans; it was the same for transport and restaurants, bars and hotels. This policy was known as segregation.

MIKHAIL GORBACHEV
RUSSIAN POLITICIAN   BORN 1931

Gorbachev went into politics when he was only 21 and quickly rose through the ranks of the Communist Party. By 1970 he was secretary of the local Party group and in 1985 he became General Secretary of the Soviet Communist Party. Aged only 54, he was the youngest for half a century to hold this senior position.

A man of vision, Gorbachev at once began to make changes. At the Geneva Summit in November 1985 he opposed the US President's 'Star Wars' policy and presented a plan to eliminate all nuclear weapons by the year 2000. A few years later saw the dismantling of the Berlin Wall which had divided east and west Berlin for almost thirty years. The USSR began to break up and all over Eastern Europe countries shook themselves free of Communist rule. In December 1991 Gorbachev was forced to resign by hard-core Communists within Russia.

KEY DATES	
1931	Gorbachev born in Privolnoye, near Stavropol, Russia
1952	Takes up politics
1970	Secretary of local Party group
1985	Leader of the USSR
1991	Forced to resign

LECH WALESA Polish Politician Born 1943
Walesa was first in the news as the leader and spokesman of the Gdansk shipyard workers in Poland and was the chairman of the strike committee in 1970. He was regarded as the 'hero of Gdansk' and co-founded the Solidarity independent trade union, and was its chairman from 1980-1990. He was awarded the Nobel Peace Prize for his handling of the shipyard strikes. In 1990 the first democratic elections in Poland following communism were held, and Walesa himself stood for President. Although he was basically a shipwright rather than a parliamentarian, he

won a landslide victory in 1990. After five years of presidency, Walesa was defeated in the 1995 elections by the former communist, Aleksander Kwasniewski.

VACLAV HAVEL
CZECH POLITICIAN
BORN 1936
With the break-up of Eastern Europe Czechoslovakia threw off the yoke of Communism. Her first president in 1989 was a playwright, writer and politician, Vaclav Havel. Havel had a long and courageous opposition to Communism and in 1979 had been sentenced to four and a half years in prison for sedition. After Czechoslovakia split into two parts, Havel became President of the Czech Republic. He is considerably respected abroad, especially in Germany, and his plays are widely performed in translation.

NELSON MANDELA
SOUTH AFRICAN FREEDOM FIGHTER AND POLITICIAN
BORN 1918

Nelson Mandela, after nearly 27 years' imprisonment, became the first black State President of South Africa in 1994, following the first free elections for both blacks and whites.

As a young man Mandela trained as a lawyer, obtaining his degree through a correspondence course, and in 1944 with his special friends and colleagues, Walter Sisulu and Oliver Tambo, he founded the African National Congress (ANC) Youth League to oppose the system called *apartheid*. Apartheid prohibited blacks from mixing with whites in employment, housing, education, on the buses, in marriage, even on park benches.

After being charged with high treason in 1956, Mandela was found not guilty in 1961. But in 1962 he was again arrested and sentenced to five years' imprisonment. While in prison new charges were brought against him and he was brought from gaol to be tried for conspiracy to overthrow the government. In 1964 he was sentenced to life imprisonment.

F.W. DE KLERK BORN 1936

F.W. de Klerk became State President of South Africa in 1989 and on assuming power he immediately began shaping a new South Africa: unbanning black political organizations, talking to the ANC and stating that in the near future there would be black majority rule in the country. He committed himself to a new democratic South Africa, free from apartheid. His decision to release Nelson Mandela from prison was the beginning of the lead-up to the momentous elections four years later.

FREEDOM AND THE PRESIDENCY

A massive 'Release Mandela' campaign was started in 1982 and in 1988, to mark his 70th birthday, a 12-hour concert was broadcast to over 50 countries. In 1990 Mandela was finally released from prison and became the deputy president of the ANC (the president being Oliver Tambo). When free elections were held in 1994, he was elected South Africa's president for a five year term. His long struggle to free his country from apartheid had not been in vain.

SHARPEVILLE MASSACRE 1960

When apartheid was at its height, all blacks were required to carry passes to restrict their movements. They had to show these passes to those in authority whenever demanded and the punishments for not carrying a pass were severe.

On 21 March 1960 there were wide but peaceful anti-pass protests by blacks. In the township of Sharpeville the police fired on men, women and children running away from them and 69 were killed, provoking world-wide outrage.

KEY DATES	
1918	Mandela born in Qumu in the Transkei, South Africa
1944	Founding of ANC Youth League
1964	Sentenced to life imprisonment
1990	Released from prison
1994	Elected President of South Africa

ARCHIMEDES
GREEK MATHEMATICIAN
AND INVENTOR c. 287–212 BC

A brilliant mathematician and inventor, Archimedes applied his mathematical skills to solving practical, everyday problems. He discovered that every object has a centre of gravity and he proved that it is possible to move a great weight with only a small force. Using a system of levers and pulleys, people could move objects many times larger and heavier than themselves. One of his famous inventions is the Archimedes Screw: it consists of a screw sealed inside a pipe which is placed in water. At the top end of the pipe is a handle which turns the blades of the screw, thus drawing water up through the pipe.

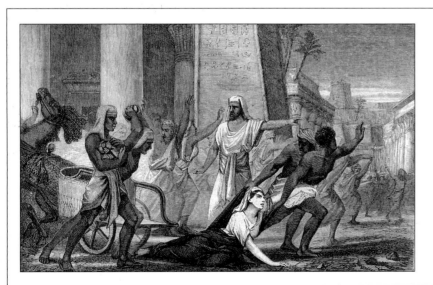

EUREKA!
The most famous story surrounding Archimedes concerns the time when King Hiero of Syracuse, suspecting that his new crown was not made of pure gold, asked Archimedes to find out if his suspicions were correct. But Archimedes was not to damage the crown.

Archimedes puzzled over this for some time, until one day when stepping into the bath he noticed that the water overflowed as he sat down. Jumping out of the bath, he ran naked through the streets, shouting 'Eureka!' (I've found it!) If the crown were made of pure gold it would take up the same amount of space in a jar of water as a piece of gold of equal weight. When Archimedes did this test with the king's crown he found that the amount of space taken up was different. The king's suspicions were correct: he had been cheated.

HYPATIA AD 370–415
Hypatia lived in Alexandria in Egypt at a time when there was fighting between the Christian community and those who followed ancient Greek beliefs. Like her father, Hypatia taught mathematics and philosophy at Alexandria's famous university. She wrote books and gave lectures. She invented a way of measuring how far stars were from the Earth, and a machine for purifying water.

Many early Christians regarded science and mathematics as pagan and there were several riots in Alexandria between Christians and non-Christians. During one of these riots Hypatia was murdered by a mob of Christians. Her body and all her books were burnt.

JOHANNES GUTENBERG
GERMAN INVENTOR OF PRINTING   c. 1398–1468

Before Gutenberg, books were either written by hand or printed using wood blocks. Gutenberg had the brilliant idea of making tiny metal blocks called 'types' – one for each letter of the alphabet. They looked like dice or scrabble tiles. Gutenberg mass-produced each piece of type from a mould, laying the pieces in racks to make words, and lined up the racks to print pages.

The lining-up work was slow, but once it was finished he could print many pages every hour. What was so important about Gutenberg's process was the possibility of making corrections so that every copy was identical.

PRINTING PRESS
Gutenberg's printing press was based on the wine presses the Romans had brought to his native Rhineland a thousand years earlier. Gutenberg's press remained in use, without any major improvements, for 300 years.

METAL TYPE
Not only did Gutenberg devise the actual printing of books and pamphlets, but he realized the individual letters would have to be available in very large numbers to print even one page. He worked out how each letter could be cast in a mould so that they were all identical and also could be picked up with ease by the printer.

Gutenberg's other invention was to make an ink which would stick to his metal type – it had to be very different from the ink used when printing from wood blocks.

BUSINESS PROBLEMS
Johannes Fust, a lawyer, lent Gutenberg money to develop his invention. Then Fust demanded his money back, and took Gutenberg's printing presses and materials. It was a sad fate for the man who made one of the most important inventions in human history.

KEY DATES

c. 1398	Gutenberg born in Mainz, Germany
1434	Works as a goldsmith in Strassburg (now Strasbourg, France)
1448	Starts printing business with Fust
1455	Loses lawsuit against Fust and is financially ruined
1468	Dies, aged about 70

WILLIAM CAXTON
c. 1422–91
Caxton is the father of printing in England. He helped to produce the first book printed in English, the *History of Troy*, and later, having gone to Cologne in Germany to study printing, he set up his own press. He produced many old popular tales, including the stories of King Arthur and tales from Chaucer.

BI SHENG
Three centuries before Gutenberg, the Chinese craftsman Bi Sheng used baked clay blocks to print playing cards, but he never made type, or printed words. From China, too, had come the invention of paper, essential when printing many copies of the same page.

GALILEO GALILEI
ITALIAN SCIENTIST 1564–1642

Galileo taught mathematics at Pisa University. Many of his studies challenged the ideas that people had believed for centuries and he became so unpopular that he was forced to leave Pisa.

Galileo agreed with the astronomical theory of Copernicus (see below) that the Earth revolved round the Sun. But the Church taught that the Earth was the centre of the Universe, and when Galileo published a book setting out his theory he was brought before the Court and, under threat of torture, forced to take back his opinions. He was denied freedom of movement and told to teach his theory no more.

Galileo was the first truly modern scientist who set out to prove his theories in a scientific manner.

THE SUN AND THE EARTH
When Galileo left Pisa, he moved to Padua. There he worked with a recent new invention, the telescope. He had the idea of focusing it on the sky. He was the first person to see Jupiter's moons and the mountains and plains of our Moon.

A century earlier, the Polish scientist, Nicolaus Copernicus (1473–1543), had said that the Sun, not the Earth, was at the centre of our solar system. Until then, everyone had thought that the Earth was the centre of the Universe and that the Sun, Moon, planets and stars revolved round it. Copernicus decided from his astronomical observations that the Earth had two movements: 1) revolving on its own axis every 24 hours, and 2) circling the Sun once a year. He published a book setting out this theory in 1543, the year of his death.

COPERNICUS

OLD WAYS AND NEW WAYS
Nowadays, scientists ask questions and test ideas all the time. In Galileo's time, tradition was important. If people had believed something for centuries, it was risky to challenge it, even if you could prove that your ideas were correct.

KEY DATES	
1473	Copernicus born in Poland
1543	Copernicus dies, aged 70
1564	Galileo born in Pisa, Italy
1589	Professor at Pisa University
1592	Professor at Padua University
1609	Begins work in astronomy
1616	In trouble for supporting Copernicus
1642	Galileo dies, aged 78

CHARLES BABBAGE
ENGLISH INVENTOR   1792–1871

Babbage enjoyed solving problems and thought he could invent a machine which would solve mathematical calculations more quickly than he could do them himself. After he had made his first 'engine', he tried to raise money to build another, bigger one that would be capable of working out much more complex problems. But the money was never available.

Babbage had no idea that about 170 years later his 'engine' would be in every school, factory, office, shop and many homes: it was the ancestor of the computer.

THE DIFFERENCE ENGINE

Babbage called his first machine a 'difference engine' ('counting machine'). It could correctly calculate simple sums time after time, without becoming tired or bored (as a human might).

Babbage was excited by the possibilities of more complicated calculating machines, and started planning a much bigger one, which he called an 'analytical engine', that would be capable of solving more complex mathematical problems.

TRANSISTORS

Babbage's 'engines' made calculations by using cogs, spindles and drive-chains. The first electronic computers used valves, but modern computers became possible in 1948, when transistors were invented by a team of scientists: William B. Shockley, John Bardeen and W. H. Brattain. Instead of chains and cogs, the transistor uses a flow of electrons.

Today, a machine the size of a credit card does work which, in Babbage's day, would have needed an 'engine' – if one could have been built – big enough to fill a tennis court.

ADA LOVELACE 1815–52

The daughter of the poet, Lord Byron, and Anne Isabella Milbanke, a mathematician, Lovelace studied mathematics, music, astronomy and languages. When she was 18 she heard Babbage describe his calculating machine. Lovelace worked out a series of step-by-step instructions for the machine, and produced the world's first computer program. In 1977, 125 years after her death, the US army called their new computer programming language ADA in her honour.

KEY DATES

1792	Babbage born in Devon, England
1823	Begins work on 'difference engine'
1828	Becomes professor of mathematics at Cambridge University
1835	Starts to plan 'analytical engine'
1871	Dies, aged 79

ISAMBARD KINGDOM BRUNEL
ENGLISH ENGINEER   1806–59

Brunel's engineering career began by helping his father, building a tunnel under the River Thames in London. In 1833 merchants in the city of Bristol wanted a railway to link London and Bristol, and they chose young Brunel's design, which he claimed would be 'not the cheapest, but the best'. The Great Western Railway was opened in 1846 with Queen Victoria riding in one of the carriages.

In 1837 Brunel's steamship, the *Great Western*, was launched. Driven by paddle power it crossed the Atlantic far more quickly than a sailing vessel. His most famous ship, the *Great Eastern* (below), at the time the biggest iron ship to be built, was launched in 1858. Although a triumph of engineering, its huge size made it difficult to manoeuvre.

Today Brunel is best remembered for his bridges the Clifton Suspension Bridge, slung on cables and steel wires over the Avon gorge in Bristol, and the Royal Albert Bridge over the River Tamar near Plymouth. Both of these bridges are still in use.

The **ROCKET** *of M.ʳ Robᵗ Stephenson of Newcastle.*
Which drawing a load equivalent to threetimes its weight travelled at the rat of 12½ miles an hour, & with a carriage & passengers at the rate of 24 miles. Cost per mile for fuel about three-halfpence.

STEAM POWER
In the eighteenth century several inventors were experimenting with steam. James Watt (1736–1819), a mathematical instrument maker at the University of Glasgow, was the first person to make an efficient steam engine which was widely used for driving factory machinery.

He continued to improve his engine, inventing further devices for it, such as a speed regulator. The unit of power, the watt, is named after him.

THE STEPHENSONS – FATHER AND SON
George Stephenson (1781–1848) began by mending the engines used to haul coal in coal mines. Eventually he decided to build one of his own, which was so successful it was still in use many years later. His most powerful engine, the *Rocket*, achieved a speed of 47 kph and was the basis of later steam engines.

George Stephenson's son, Robert (1803–59), worked with his father on the *Rocket* and was the chief engineer on the London to Birmingham railway. Robert Stephenson also built railways in Germany, Canada, Egypt and India.

KEY DATES

1769	James Watt patents his steam engine
1829	George Stephenson's *Rocket* travels at 47 kph
1831	Brunel's design for suspension bridge over River Avon accepted
1837	Brunel launches *Great Western*
1858	Brunel launches *Great Eastern*

CHARLES DARWIN
ENGLISH SCIENTIST 1809–82

In 1832 Charles Darwin was 23 – he had a degree in divinity and was also a naturalist. He had been sent on a surveying voyage on HMS *Beagle* (see below) which spent five years sailing round the world. In the Amazon rainforests he found more species of beetle than he had thought possible. When the expedition came to the archipelago of Galapagos, Darwin began to question what he had been taught – that every thing is made by God. For in Darwin's time most people believed that nothing had changed since the day of creation. From his researches on the Galapagos and elsewhere Darwin worked out his theory of evolution and published it in his book *On The Origin of Species by Means of Natural Selection* in 1859.

DARWIN'S THEORY OF EVOLUTION

What Darwin found on the Galapagos Islands led him to question his earlier beliefs, for he discovered that on each island the creatures were slightly different from the creatures on other islands. The beaks of the finches varied from island to island, according to the type of food supply, which also varied according to the terrain (landscape) of the individual islands. These differences meant that the birds had adapted to their environment, which gave them a better chance of survival. This process is known as evolution. Over millions of years some species evolve and survive; others become extinct. Evolution never stops: everything alive is evolving.

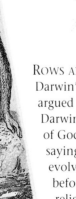

ROWS AND FIGHTS

Darwin's ideas caused a sensation. People argued and even fought about them for years. Darwin was accused of denying the existence of God. He made the situation worse by saying that apes and humans may have evolved from a single ancestor. It was years before people accepted his ideas – some religious believers still reject them.

KEY DATES	
1809	Darwin born in Shrewsbury, England
1831	HMS *Beagle* departs for South America and the Galapagos Islands
1859	First speaks publicly about evolution; publishes *On The Origin of Species*; public row begins
1882	Dies, aged 73

THOMAS EDISON
US INVENTOR   1847–1931

Edison had very little schooling – his mother took him out of school because he was beaten for asking too many questions. He started work when he was 12. One day, after he had saved a small child's life by pulling him away from an approaching rail wagon, the child's father offered to teach Edison how to tap out telegraph messages. Soon Edison had a job as a telegraph operator on a Canadian railway, and he quickly invented a better way of doing it.

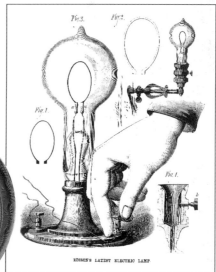

EDISON'S LATEST ELECTRIC LAMP

Edison's busy mind was constantly inventing new machines and working out improvements on old ones. One of his most original inventions was the phonograph (right), or record player, which at first he used for recording telegraph messages automatically. He also devised an electric light bulb, small enough to be used in the home, that would not burn out quickly.

ALEXANDER GRAHAM BELL
1847–1922

Bell was a Scotsman who moved to the United States when he was 23. He was a speech therapist and also a teacher of deaf children. He devised various ways of helping the deaf to speak which led to his invention of the telephone. The first telephone company, the Bell Telephone Company, was established in 1877. In 1892 Bell demonstrated the use of the telephone to businessmen by calling Chicago from New York (see above). Later in his life he was frequently involved in lawsuits brought by men who claimed they had invented the telephone before he had (including Thomas Edison).

'THE CHIEF'
'The Chief', as Edison's staff at his 'invention factory' called him, worked tirelessly at inventing. He filled 25,000 notebooks with ideas and research notes, and often went without sleep when he felt he was on to something. His 'factory' produced over 1,300 new inventions, many still in use today.

SOME KEY INVENTIONS	
1868	New telegraph system
1874	The typewriter
1877	The phonograph
1879	The electric light bulb
1888	Film camera produced by Edison's 'invention factory'
1914	Phonograph and camera connected by Edison to make 'talking' pictures

MARIE AND PIERRE CURIE
FRENCH SCIENTISTS 1867–1934 AND 1859–1906

Marie Curie was born Manya Sklodowska, in Poland. Her father, a schoolmaster, encouraged her to love learning. When she was 24 she went to Paris, where she studied in the greatest poverty. In Paris she met Pierre Curie and they married in 1895. Together they studied radiation – invisible streams of energy given off by many substances. Marie, the chemist, and Pierre, the physicist, made one of the greatest scientific partnerships ever known. Pierre discovered exact ways of measuring the energy and Marie experimented to find which substances were radioactive. In 1903 they were jointly awarded the Nobel Prize for physics and Pierre was made a professor at the University of Paris. Sadly in 1906 he was killed in a street accident and Marie succeeded him as professor – the first woman professor at the university.

HARD WORK
All her life Marie Sklodowska Curie worked extremely hard. When she was first married she taught in a girls' school to earn money so that she and her husband could continue their research. By 1911 her studies in radioactivity brought her a second Nobel Prize, this time in chemistry. Many countries honoured her with awards, and when she visited the United States or Britain she was treated like royalty.

A DRAUGHTY SHED
When the Curies were doing their important research they were desperately poor, unknown, and the parents of a little girl. Marie's first laboratory was an old storeroom at the university. Later they worked in a draughty shed, with no floor and a leaking roof. It wasn't until they received the Nobel Prize that they had a proper laboratory.

KEY DATES

1859	Pierre Curie born		jointly win Nobel Prize
1867	Marie Curie born in Warsaw, Poland	**1906**	Pierre Curie dies, aged 47; Marie Curie becomes first woman professor (of physics) in France
1886	Works as a governess to earn money		
1891	Marie Curie enrolls at Paris University	**1911**	Marie Curie wins second Nobel Prize
1896	Begins to study radiation	**1934**	Marie Curie dies, aged 67
1903	Marie and Pierre Curie		

MARIE CURIE'S BLUE FLASK
Marie Curie worked with very high levels of radiation. Radioactive particles 'irritate' certain substances, making them give off visible light particles. The glass appears blue because of this.

GUGLIELMO MARCONI
ITALIAN INVENTOR   1874–1937

As a young man, Marconi was fascinated by the newly discovered radio waves (electrical pulses in the air). He wondered if they could be used to send messages.

Until then, telegraph messages could only be sent if they passed along wires. Marconi's radio transmissions needed no wires, so he called his invention 'wireless telegraphy' or 'wireless'. Marconi's fame was made when his wireless equipment brought rescue ships to the sinking ocean liners, *Republic* and *Titanic*. Today, radio transmissions are used for communications of every kind, from entertainment to messages to and from spacecraft. We can even send radio waves into the universe and bounce them off objects far beyond our galaxy.

TRANSMITTING AND RECEIVING
Marconi worked in his father's attic, experimenting with ways to transmit (send) and receive (pick up) the waves. He made them travel along a table, across the attic, out into the garden and up a hill. There, Marconi's brother fired a gun to show that the message had arrived.

HOW FAR WILL THEY GO?
In 1896 the British Post Office gave Marconi money for research. He began to transmit messages across longer and longer distances. In 1899 he sent a message 40 km across the English Channel. In 1901 he sent a message 3,600 km across the Atlantic from Britain to Canada.

JOHN LOGIE BAIRD
1888–1946
A Scottish engineer, Baird was a pioneer in the invention of television. In 1927 he sent an image between London and Glasgow using telephone lines, and in 1928 between London and New York by radio. He made experimental TV broadcasts for the BBC from 1929 to 1937.

KEY DATES	
1874	Marconi born in Bologna, Italy
1894	First experiments
1896	Travels to Britain
1899	Sends message across English Channel
1901	First transatlantic transmission
1909	Wins Nobel Prize for Physics
1937	Dies, aged 63

ALEXANDER FLEMING
SCOTTISH SCIENTIST 1881–1955

Of all 20th century discoveries, that of penicillin is one of the most dramatic. Fleming discovered it accidentally in 1928 when he noticed that some bacteria on a culture dish in his laboratory had been killed by a mould. He then grew the mould in a liquid and observed that it prevented bacteria from growing in test tubes. His published results of his findings were largely neglected for ten years.

HOWARD FLOREY 1898–1968

Florey (right), an Australian, came to England in 1921 to study. In 1935 he was made professor of pathology at Oxford University and in 1939 he and Ernst B. Chain started to investigate the penicillin mould discovered by Fleming in 1928. After making a concentrated mould, they tested it on mice which had previously been given a fatal dose of bacteria. The mice lived. Soon it was clear that penicillin could save lives, and people who would otherwise have died from their infections lived. During the Second World War, penicillin was administered as fast as it could be produced to prevent the spread of bacterial infection and to save lives.

Because the development of penicillin happened in wartime, there were very few resources available to aid research, and Florey had to use anything he could find, like dairy equipment and bedpans, to produce penicillin in sufficient quantities.

LOUIS PASTEUR 1822–95

Pasteur was a French scientist who showed that bacteria can live almost anywhere, but their spread can be controlled by heat. He discovered that wine went sour from bacteria in the air and he saved the wine industry by applying gentle heat, thus killing the bacteria. This process is known as *pasteurization* and is also used to preserve milk and beer.

PENICILLIN

Penicillin is a powerful drug and is widely used to treat various diseases caused by bacteria. Pneumonia, rheumatic fever, and throat and ear infections have been successfully treated with penicillin. Some penicillins are given in tablet form and others in the form of injection. Unfortunately it has been found that after a few years some bacteria become resistant to penicillin and a new form of penicillin has to be developed.

KEY DATES	
1881	Fleming born in Scotland
1928	Notices the killing power of the penicillin mould
1945	Nobel Prize for Medicine shared with Howard Florey and Ernst B. Chain
1955	Dies, aged 74

CHENG HO (ALSO KNOWN AS ZHENG HE)
CHINESE EXPLORER 1371–1435

In 1405 the Chinese Emperor Ch'eng-tsu decided to send explorers west, to visit new countries and make new friends for China. To lead the expedition, he chose the finest sailor in China: Cheng Ho.

AMBASSADOR OF PEACE
Cheng Ho set sail with 62 ships and 28,000 sailors. He carried shiploads of gifts for foreign rulers: silk, porcelain, carved jade. The expedition took two years, and Cheng Ho brought back traveller's tales of fascinating cities and unusual western ways.

MAPS AND CHARTS
In the next 25 years, Cheng Ho made six more expeditions. He visited 37 different countries, sailing across the Southern Sea and the Indian Ocean to Africa. Wherever he went, he drew charts and maps of the seas and lands he visited – some of the first ever made.

MARCO POLO
1254–1324
In Marco Polo's time Venice was the most important trading centre in Europe. Believing that there was better business further east, Marco Polo's father and uncle travelled as far as China, where they met the great Kublai Khan (see p.9). Marco went with them on the next trip and the Khan offered him a post in his government. For the next 17 years Marco Polo remained in China, holding several important posts. Later he wrote a book describing the sumptuous court of Kublai Khan and his own travels in China.

JAMES COOK
The English explorer James Cook (1728–79) sailed to the Southern Ocean, visiting vast areas unknown to Europeans: Australia, New Zealand, Antarctica, and mapping their coastlines. He also sailed west, exploring the St Lawrence River in Canada. His voyages took months, and he prevented his crew catching scurvy or dysentery by insisting on cleanliness and a healthy diet. He was an excellent sailor and entirely fearless. Sadly, he was killed by Hawaiian islanders as a result of a sudden quarrel.

KEY DATES	
1371	Cheng Ho born in Yunnan, China
1378	Becomes a servant of the Emperor
1405	First expedition
1431	Last expedition
1435	Dies, aged about 64

CHRISTOPHER COLUMBUS
ITALIAN EXPLORER   1451–1506

Columbus believed that if he sailed west across the Atlantic Ocean from Europe, he would eventually come to the eastern shores of Asia, and the riches that Marco Polo had discovered there two centuries earlier. He believed that he could find an alternative route to the Spice Islands, where the precious spices used by Europeans were grown. (These islands are known today as the Molucca Islands, and up to the late 1400s they could be reached only by travelling overland eastwards from Europe.)

Columbus had to find someone to sponsor an expedition of this size. At length, after a seven-year search, Queen Isabella and King Ferdinand of Spain agreed to give him their backing.

'LAND AHOY!'
Columbus set sail in 1492, west into the Atlantic. After 65 days his sailors were ready to mutiny – but in the nick of time the lookout sighted land. The sailors had not reached Asia, as Columbus hoped, but the Bahamas in the Caribbean, alongside the continent of North America.

DID COLUMBUS DISCOVER AMERICA?
No. People had lived there for centuries before he arrived. He was the first recorded European to reach the continent. Later, another explorer, Amerigo Vespucci, claimed to have reached America first – and Europeans named the continent after him. Historians believe that the Vikings, who lived around AD 800–1100, were the first Europeans to visit North America, though they did not settle there.

VASCO DA GAMA c. 1469–1524
Spices (cloves, cinnamon, nutmeg) were important to Europeans because they flavoured and preserved food. But when the Turks captured Constantinople in 1453, the overland route to the Spice Islands was cut off and a sea route via India became vital.

Leaving Portugal in 1497, Vasco da Gama was the first to sail down the coast of Africa and round the Cape of Good Hope to India, although the voyage across the Indian Ocean took four months. At length in 1499 he arrived back in Portugal with the first seaborne cargo of spices from the east. A sea route to India was now established.

KEY DATES	
1451	Columbus born in Genoa, Italy
1485	Begins raising money
1492	Sails west; lands on island in Bahamas, probably San Salvador
1506	Dies, aged 55

MERIWETHER LEWIS AND WILLIAM CLARK
AMERICAN EXPLORERS
1774–1809 AND 1770–1838

Lewis and Clark were army officers and friends. At the time, nearly 200 years ago, white people knew only a small section of the huge lands that were to become part of the United States. President Jefferson asked Lewis to lead an expedition into the unknown areas, and Lewis asked Clark to join him.

The president told Lewis and Clark to travel from St Louis up the Missouri River to the Pacific Ocean. On the way they were to draw maps, and to write notes about animals, plants and scenery. Above all, they were to make friends with the local peoples, many of whom had never seen a white person before.

THERE AND BACK AGAIN
Lewis and Clark walked over 2,000 kilometres and met several native tribes on their expedition. The native Americans were mostly friendly towards them, partly because Lewis and Clark usually had several native people with them. They spent the winter in Oregon on the Pacific coast, and then started back. They split into two parties. Lewis had a difficult journey. He suffered from fever, was attacked by the hostile Blackfoot tribe, from whom he was forced to flee, and was accidentally shot by one of his own men. However, after two years, both men arrived back safely to a hero's welcome.

AFTERWARDS
People were fascinated by the tales Lewis and Clark told of the 'Wild West', and many decided to go there and see for themselves. Lewis and Clark planned to go back one day too. After Lewis' death in 1809, Clark spent 17 years working with the native people.

KEY DATES	
1770	William Clark born
1774	Meriwether Lewis born
1804	Expedition sets out in May
1806	Expedition returns in September
1809	Lewis killed, aged 35
1838	Clark dies, aged 68

SIMON BOLIVAR
SOUTH AMERICAN GENERAL   1783–1830

When Símon Bolívar was young, Spain controlled most countries in South America. When he grew up he became a soldier and vowed to set these countries free. His chance came in 1808, when Napoleon invaded Spain. The Spanish army was pinned down in Europe, defending its own country. In South America, Bolívar gathered soldiers and marched on the attack.

Without their army to support them, the Spanish settlers in South America were no match for Bolívar and his army. He liberated (set free) Venezuela, Colombia and Ecuador. Other generals freed other states, and one state (northern Peru) was renamed Bolivia to honour Bolívar.

OTHER FREEDOM FIGHTERS
Two other generals worked with Bolívar to free their countries from Spanish rule. The half-Irish Bernardo O'Higgins (1778–1842) liberated Chile, and later became its first president. The Argentinian José de San Martín (1778–1850), having liberated his own country, turned to Peru and occupied Lima, the capital, but he was not strong enough to evict the Spaniards completely, so had to ask Bolívar for help.

JOSE DE SAN MARTIN

A UNITED COUNTRY
Bolívar wanted to merge all the countries he had liberated into one large country, with a single ruler (himself). That way, he said, the new country would be too strong for Spain, or any other country, to conquer. The people Bolívar had liberated resisted. They were loyal to their own small countries, and didn't want a kingdom the size of half a continent. There were revolts, one after another, in all the liberated countries, and Bolívar fell ill and died before his dream could come true, but all over South America, he is still remembered as 'The Liberator', and his statue stands in many towns.

TOUSSAINT L'OUVERTURE 1743–1803
A negro ex-slave, Toussaint L'Ouverture was one of the liberators of San Domingo (now Haiti) in the West Indies and he became the island's first governor.

San Domingo was ruled partly by France and partly by Spain and when the French gave the negroes equal rights with whites there was revolt and tumult on the island. Later the French made Toussaint commander in chief of a large force, and by 1800 the whole of the French part of the island was under his control. In 1801 he seized the Spanish part as well. But Napoleon hated Toussaint and, declaring that slavery must be re-established, sent an army of 25,000 men against Toussaint, who was taken prisoner. He died in a French dungeon.

KEY DATES	
1783	Bolívar born in Caracas, Venezuela
1798	Travels in Europe
1810	Begins revolution in Venezuela
1819-21	Liberates Venezuela, Colombia and Ecuador
1828	Escapes assassination
1830	Dies of tuberculosis, aged 47

DAVID LIVINGSTONE
SCOTTISH MEDICAL MISSIONARY AND EXPLORER 1813-73

Having qualified as a doctor and medical missionary, David Livingstone was sent to Botswana (then Bechuanaland) in 1840. While working there over a period of ten years, he became convinced that it was his duty to explore the vast territories of central Africa and open routes, not only for other missionaries, but also for trade.

In 1858 Livingstone was commissioned by the British government to explore eastern and central Africa. On this trip he discovered Lake Nyasa. He also entered an area almost devastated by the slave trade and became increasingly determined that something must be done to stamp out this horrible trade in human beings.

In 1866 Livingstone set out on another expedition, partly to carry on the fight against the slave trade, but also to find the source of the Nile. He travelled vast distances and suffered dreadful hardships, especially after the theft of his medicine chest deprived him of the means of controlling his fever. He was almost given up for lost, but an American newspaper organised an expedition under H.M. Stanley to find him. In November 1871 the two men met on the eastern shore of Lake Tanganyika, with the now famous greeting 'Dr Livingstone, I presume?'

Livingstone's health had been badly damaged by the hardships of his long journey and on 2nd May 1873 his servants found him dead. They carried him and his precious journals over 1,500 km back to Zanzibar. His body was then taken to London and he is buried in Westminster Abbey.

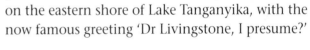

KEY DATES	
1813	Livingstone born in Blantyre, Scotland
1823	Begins working in a cotton mill but educates himself in the evenings
1844	Marries Mary Moffat
1853	Livingstone begins his first trek and becomes first European to cross Africa from East to West
1873	Livingstone dies, aged 60

MARY KINGSLEY English Explorer 1862-1900
Until she was 30, Mary Kingsley looked after her younger brother and her mother who was constantly ill. Her father was a doctor who spent most of his time abroad, and Mary became fascinated by the places he described in his letters. In 1893, after both her parents died, Mary went to West Africa to learn about the natural history of the region. She also became very interested in the customs and culture of the African people she met. After a period in Britain, during which time she published her journals and gave lectures about her experiences of life on the 'dark continent', Mary returned to Africa. This time she travelled to South Africa where she nursed British soldiers fighting in the Boer War until her death in 1900.

FRIDTJOF NANSEN 1861–1930
ROALD AMUNDSEN 1872–1928
NORWEGIAN POLAR EXPLORERS

In the extreme north of the world lies a freezing ocean, the Arctic Ocean, and in the south is a frozen continent, Antarctica. They are dangerous places for ships and men – the sea is full of treacherous icebergs and in the winter it is frozen solid; the land at the South Pole is a mass of snowfields, frozen mountains and deep crevasses which can swallow up a whole team of dogs and men.

For many years Europeans hoped to find a new route to the Pacific Ocean by going north, but the Arctic winter always defeated them.

FRIDTJOF NANSEN
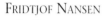
In the summer of 1888 Nansen, a Norwegian, crossed Greenland with five companions – a feat previously declared impossible. He was determined to explore the polar seas and had a ship, the *Fram*, especially built to withstand the dangerous ice floes. After spending two years on the ship, he and one other tried to reach the North Pole with sledges. Although they did not reach the Pole, their journey taught them a great deal about polar exploration that was valuable to future explorers.

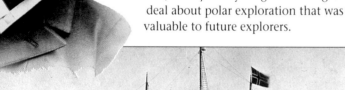

ROALD AMUNDSEN
Another Norwegian, Amundsen, wanted to be the first to reach the North Pole, but just before he set out he learned that an American, Robert E. Peary, had got there already. So he changed his plans and decided to go to the South Pole instead. He left Norway secretly in June 1910. At the same time a party of British explorers under the command of Captain Robert Scott was also on its way to the South Pole. It was now a race for the Pole.

SCOTT AND THE RACE FOR THE SOUTH POLE
Amundsen had only four men, four sledges and dogs to pull them. When some of the dogs weakened, they were killed and their bodies fed to the others. Scott took more men, dogs, sledges, snow tractors and ponies, but when the ponies were exhausted, the men had to pull the sledges carrying the supplies themselves. Amundsen made better time; he had chosen a slightly shorter and easier route, and on 14th December 1911 he reached the South Pole.

When Scott's party arrived five weeks later (see left), they found the Norwegian flag already in place. On their return journey to base camp, the whole of Scott's party died during a blizzard.

KEY DATES	
1895	Nansen tries to reach North Pole
1909	Robert E. Peary reaches North Pole
Dec 1911	Amundsen reaches South Pole
Jan 1912	Scott reaches South Pole
Mar 1912	Scott's party dies on return journey

WILBUR AND ORVILLE WRIGHT
US PIONEERS OF AVIATION
1867–1912 AND 1871–1948

The Wright brothers wanted to build and to fly the first powered flying machine that was heavier than air. At last, in 1903, they flew their powered glider for the first time, although they were in the air for barely a minute. At first nobody took them very seriously, but by 1908 they had a contract with the US War Department for the first military aeroplanes.

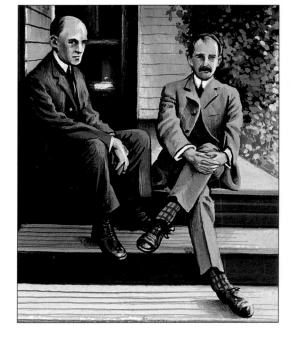

THE FIRST FLYING-MACHINE
The Wright brothers flew their first flying-machine at Kitty Hawk in the USA in December 1903. It weighed 340 kilograms, had wings 12 metres long and could reach a speed of 49 kilometres an hour. It cost less than $1,000 to build. In 1928 Orville sent the plane to the Science Museum in London, but in 1948 it was returned to the USA.

PIONEERS IN THE AIR
The early aviators were brave. There were many crashes and pilots often died.

LOUIS BLÉRIOT (1872–1936) made the first flight over the English Channel in 1909 on a plane he had built himself (see above). Luckily there was a light rain falling which cooled his rapidly overheating engine.

CHARLES LINDBERGH (1902–74) was the first pilot to fly across the Atlantic on a non-stop solo flight. He made his historic 3,600 mile flight on 10–11th May 1927, flying from New York to Paris in 33 1/2 hours.

In 1930 AMY JOHNSON (1903–41) was the first woman to fly solo from Britain to Australia. It took her 15 days.

In 1932 AMELIA EARHART (1898–1937) flew solo across the Atlantic Ocean, and five years later she attempted a round-the-world flight, but her plane crashed and she disappeared.

AMY JOHNSON

FRANK WHITTLE 1907–96
Whittle worked in the British Royal Air Force in the 1930s. At that time, planes were all driven by piston engines (like enormous car engines) which powered propellers. Whittle invented the jet engine: producing movement in one direction by releasing a high-pressure stream of gas in the opposite direction. Jet engines now power every kind of plane as well as rockets and guided missiles.

KEY DATES			
1903	Wright brothers fly first aeroplane	**1919**	John Alcock and Arthur Brown make non-stop transatlantic flight
1909	Blériot flies across English Channel	**1927**	Lindbergh flies solo from New York to Paris
1911/12	Aeroplanes first used for bombing raids		

YURI GAGARIN
RUSSIAN COSMONAUT   1934–68

Gagarin, a pilot with the Soviet Air Force, volunteered in 1959 as a trainee cosmonaut with the Soviet space programme When the spaceship *Vostok I* was ready, Gagarin was chosen to pilot it. On 12th April 1961 *Vostok I* blasted off with Gagarin aboard. It made one orbit of the Earth and landed (by parachute) 108 minutes after take-off. No human being had ever flown in space before and Gagarin was a world hero, but he was not interested in fame or fortune. In 1968 Gagarin died in a routine training flight in an ordinary plane. He was given a huge state funeral.

THE FIRST WOMAN IN SPACE
Valentina Tereshkova (b. 1937), a Russian factory worker, took up parachute jumping in 1959. After Gagarin's space flight in 1961 she volunteered to train as a cosmonaut. On 16th June 1963 her spaceship *Vostok VI* orbited the Earth 48 times. She was named 'Hero of the Soviet Union'.

WALKING ON THE MOON
Eight years after Gagarin's triumph the United States won the next big prize in the space race. In 1969 three US astronauts travelled to the Moon in the spacecraft *Apollo 11*, and while one of them stayed in the spacecraft, the others, Aldrin and Armstrong, landed on the surface of the Moon, watched by millions on television throughout the world. They left one of Gagarin's medals on the Moon to honour the first human being in space.

SALLY RIDE
Twenty years later the US scientist Sally Ride (b. 1951) became the first American woman to travel in space when she blasted off on the space shuttle *Challenger*.

THE SPACE SHUTTLE
The Space Shuttle is designed to take off like a rocket and land like an aeroplane and can carry as many as seven crew members. The shuttle is reusable – only the rockets and external fuel tank are discarded.

KEY DATES	
1957	*Sputnik I*, first satellite, launched
1961	Gagarin orbits the Earth in *Vostok I*
1969	Americans land on Moon
1973	Skylab, an experimental US space station, launched
1981	US Space Shuttle makes first flight

MURASAKI SHIKIBU
JAPANESE WRITER 976–1031

Lady Murasaki lived in Japan. Art, writing and music were all very popular among Japanese noble families. Young noblewomen were taught how to compose poems and letters, do calligraphy (beautiful writing), play musical instruments and sing. Murasaki lived in the royal palace. When she was young, she started keeping a diary, making notes of all the interesting things she had seen and heard. She became expert at describing people and places. When she was older, she used these skills to help her write a book – *The Tale of Genji*. This tells the story of Prince Genji, a soldier, and of the woman he loves. *The Tale of Genji* is one of the first books written by a Japanese woman, and one of the earliest known novels (books telling a story) in the world.

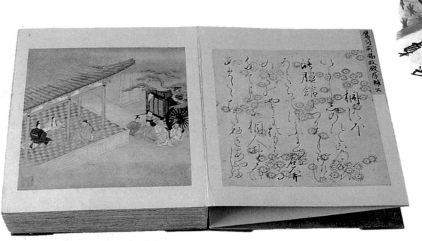

STORIES ON SILK
The Tale of Genji was written on a scroll (a long roll) of fine silk cloth. The writing was painted on to the silk using a brush. Lady Murasaki illustrated her story with pictures of the people and places described in it. Her scroll is now one of Japan's national treasures.

QUEEN MATILDA'S TAPESTRY
Queen Matilda was the wife of Duke William of Normandy – William the Conqueror – and she became Queen of England after the Battle of Hastings (1066). For many years she was believed to be the designer and chief embroiderer of what is called the Bayeux Tapestry. But it is now thought that Bishop Odo, William's half-brother, ordered the tapestry to be made for his cathedral in Bayeux, a town in Normandy, where it may still be seen – all 71 metres of it. The tapestry tells the story in wonderful embroidered pictures of the events leading up to the battle of Hastings and the death of King Harold.

LEONARDO DA VINCI
ITALIAN ARTIST   1452–1519

Leonardo began to train as an artist when he was fifteen. He learned painting, sculpture and drawing – at which he was especially talented. When his training finished, he stayed for a time in Florence, then travelled north to work at the court of the Duke of Milan.

Leonardo had several jobs while in Milan. He had to paint pictures and make sculptures. He was the Duke's adviser on fortifications and military machines. He also designed scenery and costumes for plays, ballets, pageants and other court entertainments.

When Leonardo left Milan to work for other employers, he gave up his stage work, but kept all his other interests. He also found the time to study science. Leonardo was especially interested in natural forces, such as the wind or the flow of water, and in the detailed study of plants and animals.

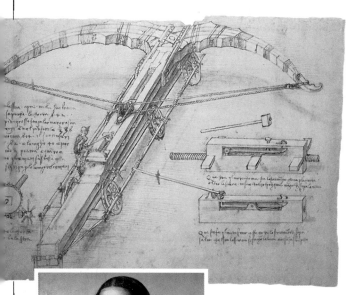

AHEAD OF HIS TIME
During his later years, Leonardo did very little painting, but revealed his genius with all things mechanical. He produced pages and pages of ideas about art, engineering and science. About 4,000 of these pages still exist and show plans for flying machines, a submarine, a giant crossbow, a movable bridge, a bike and a construction crane.

MICHELANGELO 1475–1564
Michelangelo is especially famous for his marble sculptures and for his paintings on the ceiling of the Sistine Chapel in the Vatican. His sculptures are much larger than life size and he took immense care in choosing the right piece of marble before he commenced work. The amazing details he created in the sculptures and the warmth in the expressions of the figures have never been surpassed. But he was also a painter and undertook large commissions, often from the Pope. It was Pope Julius II who asked Michelangelo to paint the Sistine Chapel ceiling – probably his greatest achievement as a painter.

KEY DATES	
1452	Leonardo born near the village of Vinci
1467	Begins training
1482	Travels to Milan to work
1500	Travels to Florence to work
1516	Travels to France to work
1519	Dies, aged 67

THE MONA LISA – Leonardo's most famous painting

JANE AUSTEN
ENGLISH NOVELIST 1775–1817
AND WRITERS OF THE NINETEENTH CENTURY

In the nineteenth century novel-writing came alive. Earlier centuries had produced fine poets and playwrights, but it was not until Jane Austen wrote such works as *Sense and Sensibility* and *Pride and Prejudice,* that readers were able to appreciate humour and the delicate way of handling characters, as well as the telling of an absorbing story.

MARK TWAIN
Mark Twain, real name Samuel Langhorne Clemens (1835–1910), the creator of Tom Sawyer and Huckleberry Finn, was one of America's major writers. *Tom Sawyer* recalls Twain's own childhood and Tom and his friend Huck are two of the most lively characters in American fiction.

At this time some women writers felt compelled to use male pen-names in order to get their work published. The three Brontë sisters, Charlotte (1816–55), Emily (1818–48) and Anne (1820–49), living in a remote parsonage on the Yorkshire moors, chose names based on their own initials: Currer (Charlotte), Ellis (Emily) and Acton (Anne) Bell. Charlotte's story, *Jane Eyre,* is partly based on her own life and describes a brave young governess who falls in love and eventually finds happiness.

Another woman who used a pen-name was Mary Ann Evans (1819–80) who called herself George Eliot. Her books, which are mostly set in the English countryside, still appear under this male name. The best known are *Silas Marner, The Mill on the Floss* and *Middlemarch.*

CHARLES DICKENS
One of the most popular of English 19th-century novelists, Dickens (1812–70) wrote many of his books in serial form and readers had to wait for the next instalment. His experiences in a London factory at the age of twelve served as a useful background for his books set among London's poor. His best-known books are *Oliver Twist, A Christmas Carol, Great Expectations* and *David Copperfield.*

In America, Harriet Beecher Stowe (1811–96) made history with her anti-slavery novel *Uncle Tom's Cabin.* This book awoke people to the evils of slavery, which was one of the causes of the American Civil War.

The nineteenth century also saw the first important horse story – *Black Beauty.* Anna Sewell (1820–78) wrote it as a protest against cruelty to horses. Although she was an invalid, she could still ride her horse and her love for it inspired this book.

Leo Tolstoy (1828–1910) was an important Russian writer who, as a young man, served in the Russian army during the Crimean War. He wrote several articles showing war to be a bloodbath and far from romantic. He is remembered for his two great novels – *War and Peace* and *Anna Karenina.*

MATTHEW BRADY
US PHOTOGRAPHER   1823–96

In 1844 the photographer Matthew Brady started a gallery of famous Americans and made a collection of daguerrotype portraits. But a daguerrotype was on metal and the exposure time was long. Later it was possible by an elaborate wet process to print pictures on paper, and at the outbreak of the American Civil War Brady decided to make a complete record of the action, bringing the reality of war home to those away from the front. He required an enormous amount of equipment and had a large photographic van on wheels. Although the project ruined him financially, his photographs are considered among the finest war pictures of all time.

It was soon realized that photography could record the realities of life more quickly than a painting, and photographers travelled all over the world, sending back remarkable pictures of dramatic scenery.

OTHER IMPORTANT PHOTOGRAPHERS

Julia Margaret Cameron (1815–79), an Englishwoman (pictured right), took up portrait photography in 1864 and produced memorable pictures of such famous people as Lord Tennyson and Charles Darwin.

In 1888 an American, George Eastman, invented the Kodak camera. These hand-held cameras, more than anything else, made photography available to everybody.

By the 20th century Henri Cartier-Bresson was well-known for being the man who took 'snapshots' using a miniature camera. He was an unseen witness, recording impressions of people spontaneously.

The American photographer Margaret Bourke-White captured both social and war history in her photographs taken before and during World War II, and she was one of the first to take pictures of the Nazi concentration camps in 1945.

LOUIS DAGUERRE (1789–1851)

In the 1830s a Frenchman, Louis Daguerre , began experimenting with a box containing a lens at one end, and by 1837 he had taken a photograph of his studio on a silvered copper plate. His name was given to the process known as a daguerrotype.

KEY DATES

1837	Louis Daguerre photographs his studio
1844	Matthew Brady starts his 'gallery of famous Americans'
1862	Brady begins his photographic record of the American Civil War
1864	Julia M. Cameron takes up portrait photography
1888	Kodak camera invented

ANDREW CARNEGIE
US STEEL MAGNATE AND BENEFACTOR   1835–1919

Born in Scotland, Carnegie and his family emigrated to the United States when Andrew was 12. The young Carnegie worked in a cotton mill, teaching himself to send and receive telegraph messages. Later, during the American Civil War, he helped organize telegraph services for the northern states.

In 1853 Carnegie was working for the Pennsylvania Railroad and began investing in several iron companies. By 1865 he was running his own business. He quickly realized the demand for steel would increase and, despite slumps in the steel industry, Carnegie's steel mills earned millions of dollars.

When Carnegie retired in 1901 he was called the 'richest man in the world'.

THE BENEFACTOR

Carnegie's greatest claim to fame can perhaps be the contribution he made to society after he retired. He donated about $350 million to various causes, and was particularly concerned that wealthy individuals should help those who were less fortunate. But he believed the help should be in the form of educational opportunities. He equipped over 3,000 public libraries in towns in the United States and Great Britain, and set up scholarships and foundations for the purposes of study. He gave $10 million to Scottish universities. He started good pension funds for his steel workers and for American university professors. In 1937 the Library Association in London established the Carnegie Medal in his name. It is given each year to the writer of an outstanding book for children.

KEY DATES	
1835	Carnegie born in Dunfermline, Scotland
1848	Emigrates to the United States
1865	Starts to run his own business
1873	Establishes steel mill near Pittsburgh
1901	Retires, the 'richest man in the world'
1919	Dies, aged 83

GEORGE CADBURY 1839–1922

At the age of 21, George Cadbury and his brother Richard took over the chocolate and cocoa business founded by their father.

George had long realized that the living conditions of the workers were appalling and in 1894 they set up a new factory about five miles from Birmingham at a place they called Bournville. There they built houses for the workforce, with gardens and plenty of space. The money made from the rents was used to improve and expand the properties. The Bournville experiment had a great influence on the garden cities of the future.

In addition, the Cadburys improved the working conditions in the factory: people were given regular time off, there were opportunities to go to night school, there were pensions, children's allowances, medical services and, above all, everyone played their part in administering these schemes. All these things are nowadays taken for granted, but in the 19th century they were remarkable.

HENRY FORD
US INDUSTRIALIST 1863–1947

As a young man, Ford worked for a lighting company in Detroit in the USA. His hobby was the new sport of motoring. In his spare time, he built his first car and soon afterwards he left the lighting company to start his own motor company.

PRODUCTION LINE
Ford's first workers were craftsmen. Each did every job needed to make a car – something like 50 different jobs. It was a slow and expensive process, so in 1913 Ford introduced the production line. Cars stood on a slowly moving conveyor belt, which passed worker after worker. Each worker did only one job – the same job – on car after car.

Working this way, the factory could make hundreds of cars each week. Ford was unpopular with his workers, but most car manufacturers still use a modernized version of his production line in their factories to this day.

CARS FOR EVERYONE
In those days, cars were expensive luxuries, only bought by the rich. Ford wanted to make cars which most people could afford. He began with the Model A and then improved it to make the Model B, and so on, as far as the Model T. The Model T was cheap and reliable, and at the time it was the most popular car ever made.

KEY DATES	
1863	Ford born in Michigan, USA
1895	Chief Engineer for the Detroit Edison Company
1896	Builds his first car
1908	Begins making the Model T Ford
1947	Dies, aged 84

BIG BUSINESS
The Ford Motor Company soon became huge. From 1908 to 1927, it made over half the cars sold each year in the USA. By 1927 more than 15 million Model Ts had been sold. The Ford Motor Company now has factories in over 50 countries worldwide and is one of the giants of American industry. It has come a long way since its beginnings in Henry Ford's workshop in a corner of his father's farm.

CLAUDE MONET
FRENCH PAINTER   1840 –1926

Claude Monet was one of the pioneers of a group that came to be called the Impressionists. Their aim was not to paint the traditional pictures popular at the time, but to portray light in its ever-changing moods and the effect it had on the landscape. Monet often painted the same scene again and again – at different times of day and in different seasons. At first, his exhibitions were a disaster and his pictures were almost given away; he was so poor he had to borrow money to keep his family. But success came at last. In the 1890s Monet painted some of his most famous 'series' pictures – haystacks and the cathedral at Rouen in varying lights. His paintings of his garden – the dazzling water with the water lilies, the trees and flowers – seem to portray paradise.

THE IMPRESSIONISTS
Because of their style of painting – small brush strokes of colour where it is your eyes that mix the colour, giving a feeling of rippling water, waving grass, dancing light, these talented artists were called Impressionists. In addition to Monet, some of the best known are Renoir and Pissarro.

JEERED AT!
After having their paintings turned down for the International Exhibition in Paris in 1863, many of the rejected artists were so furious that a special 'Show of Rejects' was arranged. The people who visited the exhibition jeered and laughed at the paintings, which were unlike any paintings they had ever seen before. But the artists gradually came to know one another – they met in cafés and, through encouragement of each other, became the most famous artists of the period.

VINCENT VAN GOGH (1853–90) was born in Holland and his early pictures depict the lives of the people in his village. In 1886 he went to stay with his brother Theo in Paris, where he met many Impressionist artists who encouraged him to use brighter colours. He later went to live in Arles in the south of France, where he painted pictures bathed in sunlight: fruit trees, his village house, sunflowers. Although his pictures now fetch millions of pounds, in his lifetime he sold only one painting.

PABLO PICASSO
SPANISH ARTIST 1881–1973

Picasso was born in Malaga in Spain and at first painted realistic pictures of ordinary people. He was exhibiting his paintings by the age of 14. When he was 23 he moved from Spain to Paris, where the big city and the lives of circus people influenced his art. In 1907 Picasso saw an exhibition of African masks. He was amazed at the shapes: human faces shown as triangles, circles, cubes and diamonds. He experimented with such shapes in his own paintings. His art was constantly responding to change and throughout his long life he experimented. He was always challenging people to look at painting in a new way, hoping that the images he portrayed would penetrate people's minds, rather as dreams and nightmares do. He is without doubt the most important artist of the 20th century.

THE ART OF PICASSO

Picasso painted hundreds of pictures using many different styles. There was the 'blue' period, which seems to depict the sadness in many people's lives. There was the 'Cubism' period, in which the picture is created out of geometrical shapes. Picasso also experimented with flat colours and lines – the painting of *The Sculptor* (above right) is an example of this style. His painting *Guernica* (right) shows the grief and rage when this small Spanish town was obliterated by bombs during the Spanish Civil War (1936–39).

HENRY MOORE 1898–1986

Henry Moore was born in Yorkshire and always wanted to be a sculptor. He became even more enthusiastic when he discovered the art and sculpture of Africa and the Aztecs in Mexico. He did not always make a sculpture that could be given a definite name, but created a powerful shape from the natural material, wood or stone, from which it was made. During the Second World War his drawings of Londoners sheltering in Underground stations soon attracted public interest. After the war he rapidly became famous for his large forms of human beings that look as if they have been beaten by the wind into a huge stone. Many of his pieces are intended to stand on hillsides where they blend with the landscape.

ANNA PAVLOVA
RUSSIAN BALLERINA
1885–1931

Born in a poor family in St Petersburg, the young Anna was taken as a treat to see the Imperial Russian Ballet. Immediately she knew she had to be a dancer, and two years later she was accepted for the Imperial Ballet School.

She was quickly spotted as having outstanding talent and when she graduated into the Ballet company was soon dancing solo roles. A few years later she began to make brief appearances outside Russia and in 1909 danced in Paris when the Russian Ballet under Diaghilev visited the city for their first dazzling season.

Pavlova realized that touring companies brought ballet to audiences who would normally never see a great ballerina and in 1913 she set up her own company with which she toured the world. Her dancing was seen by millions and some who saw her dance were themselves inspired to make dancing their career.

ISADORA DUNCAN 1877–1927
Isadora rebelled against the rigid formality of classical ballet – she felt dancing should be free and individual. She often danced in a loose tunic and bare feet and had a strong influence on dancing in the early 20th century. She based many of her dances on poetry and classical music.

SERGEI DIAGHILEV 1872–1929
Sergei Diaghilev was one of the world's most inspired directors of ballet. Born in Novgorod in Russia he established his own company, the Ballet Russe, bringing together dancers, musicians, painters and choreographers (composers of dance routines) and creating a new theatrical form of ballet. When his company visited Paris in 1909 they caused a sensation. Parisians had never seen dancing like it before. He was constantly seeking young talent, keen to make them better artists by exposing them to music and other creative artists. That his company included Pavlova, the legendary Nijinsky, Tamara Karsavina and the composer Stravinsky is a sign of his own enormous talents.

BRITISH BALLET
Two women, Dame Ninette de Valois – pictured above – (born 1898) and Dame Marie Rambert (1888–1982), have made British ballet as we know it today. Marie Rambert started the ballet company that still bears her name in 1926, the year Frederick Ashton created his first ballet. Ninette de Valois started her ballet school in 1931, and, with Ashton as choreographer, the Vic-Wells Ballet and then the great Royal Ballet grew and developed.

BILL GATES
US COMPUTER PIONEER   BORN 1955

Bill Gates showed an interest in computers from an early age. He was a bright pupil and started writing his own computer programs while he was at secondary school. In 1974, after gaining a place at Harvard University, he wrote BASIC – the computer language used to programme one of the first microcomputers, the MITS Altair. Computers were not widely used in the early seventies, but Gates was convinced that the personal computer would soon revolutionise offices and homes throughout the world. With this vision for the future, he set up a company – Microsoft – to produce software for personal computers. In 1980 Gates was approached by IBM to devise the operating system for the PC microcomputer that they were developing. Since then, Gates' MS-DOS system has become the most widely used operating system in the world and today Microsoft employs thousands of people in many countries.

OF MICE AND MEN
An American scientist called Doug Engelbart designed the first mouse in 1965 while he was working at the Stanford Research Institute. A ball on the underside of the mouse registers movements which are transmitted to the computer via a lead. These movements are then translated to the cursor on the screen. However, it was not until the user-friendly Apple Macintosh was launched in 1984 that the mouse became the familiar computer accessory that it is today.

SIR CLIVE SINCLAIR BORN 1940
Sinclair has made an important contribution to the development of personal computers in Britain. He has also invented or perfected other electronic gadgets such as the digital watch and the pocket calculator. In 1966 Sinclair designed the world's first mini-television. One of his more bizarre creations was the C5: a battery-powered one-person vehicle. Sinclair was knighted in 1983.

SPARKING OFF A REVOLUTION
The most significant development in computer technology was the invention of the microprocessor in 1971. A microprocessor is the computer's calculating and control centre. It is an integrated electronic circuit that can perform over a million operations per second. The US company, Intel, made the first microprocessors.

COMPUTER COMPETITION
Two years after IBM brought out their first personal computer, the 5100, in 1975, two young Americans were designing a machine that was to become a major rival to the IBM model. It was called the Apple II and was built by Steve Jobs and Stephen Wozniak. They used a garage as their makeshift computer lab! They went on to introduce the highly successful Macintosh computer. Until 1987 Macintosh and IBM computers were incompatible, but then a breakthrough was made that meant the two systems could use the same software.

KEY DATES

1946	J.W. Mauchly and J.P. Eckert from the USA build the first electronic computer, called ENIAC.
1950	Yoshiro Nakamats designs the first floppy disk in Tokyo. (Before the arrival of the floppy disk data was stored on reels of magnetic tape.)
1971	M. E. Hoff invents the microprocessor. It was a 4-bit processor. Today much more powerful computers use processors.
1971	François Gernelle, a French engineer, develops the first microcomputer. It is called Micral.
1972	Three scientists working in the USA patent the first pocket calculator.

INDEX

Akbar the Great, 9
Alexander the Great, 7
Amundsen, Roald, 49
Archimedes, 34
Augustus, Emperor, 8
Austen, Jane, 56

Babbage, Charles, 37
Baird, John Logie, 42
Bandaranaike, Sirimavo, 17
Beethoven, Ludwig van, 55
Bell, Alexander Graham, 40
Bhutto, Benazir, 17
Bolivar, Simon, 47
Brady, Matthew, 57
Brunel, Isambard Kingdom, 38

Cadbury, George, 58
Calvin, John, 21
Carnegie, Andrew, 58
Catherine the Great, 12
Caxton, William, 35
Churchill, Winston, 15
Clark, William, 46
Cleopatra, 8
Columbus, Christopher, 45
Cook, James, 44
Copernicus, Nicolaus, 36
Curie, Marie and Pierre, 41

Daguerre, Louis, 57
Darwin, Charles, 39
Davison, Emily, 27
Diaghilev, Sergei, 62
Dickens, Charles, 56
Duncan, Isadora, 62

Edison, Thomas, 40
Elizabeth I, 11

Fleming, Alexander, 43
Florey, Howard, 43
Ford, Henry, 59
Froebel, Friedrich, 28
Fry, Elizabeth, 22

Gagarin, Yuri, 51
Galilei, Galileo, 36
Gama, Vasco da, 45
Gandhi, Indira, 17
Gandhi, Mohandas Karmachand, 30
Gates, Bill, 63
Gautama, Siddhartha, (the Buddha), 18
Genghis Khan, 9
Gorbachev, Mikhail, 32
Gutenberg, Johannes, 35

Havel, Vaclav, 32
Henry VIII, 21
Hitler, Adolf, 15
Ho, Cheng, 44
Hypatia, 34

Jacobs, Aletta, 29
Jesus Christ, 19
Joan of Arc, 10
Julius Caesar, 8

King, Martin Luther, 31
Kingsley, Mary, 48
Klerk, F W de, 33
Kublai Kahn, 9

Lenin, Vladimir Ilyich, 26
Leonardo da Vinci, 53
Lewis, Meriwether, 46
Lincoln, Abraham, 14
Livingstone, David, 48
Lovelace, Ada, 37
Luther, Martin, 21

Mandela, Nelson, 33
Mao Ze Dong, 16
Marconi, Guglielmo, 42
Marx, Karl, 26
Matilda (of Normandy), Queen, 52
Meir, Golda, 17
Michelangelo, 53
Monet, Claude, 60
Montessori, Maria, 28
Moore, Henry, 61
Moses, 6

Mozart, Wolfgang Amadeus, 55
Muhammad, 20

Nanak, Guru, 20
Nansen, Fridtjof, 49
Napoleon Bonaparte, 13
Nelson, Horatio, 13
Nightingale, Florence, 24

Pankhurst, Emmeline, 27
Pasteur, Louis, 43
Pavlova, Anna, 62
Peter the Great, 12
Picasso, Pablo, 61
Polo, Marco, 44

Ride, Sally, 51

Sanger, Margeret, 29
Schumann, Clara, 55
Scott, Robert, 49
Seacole, Mary, 24
Shakespeare, William, 54
Shikibu, Murasaki, 52
Sinclair, Clive, 63
Stanton, Elizabeth Cady, 23
Stephenson, George and Robert, 38
Stopes, Marie, 29
Stuart, Miranda, 22

Tamerlane, 9
Teresa, Mother, 24
Tereshkova, Valentina, 51
Toussaint L'Ouverture, 47
Truth, Sojourner, 25
Tubman, Harriet, 25

Van Gogh, Vincent, 60

Walesa, Lech, 32
Washington, George, 14
Watt, James, 38
Whittle, Frank, 50
Wollstonecraft, Mary, 22
Woodhull, Victoria, 23
Wright brothers, The, 50

ACKNOWLEDGEMENTS

PHOTOGRAPHS
Associated Press: 15t; Bridgeman Art Library: 6b, 7b, 8c, 10b, 11b, 18t, 19t, 19c, 20t, 35b, 39cr, 43b, 45t, 45c, 45b, 48c, 52b, 53c, 53bl, 53br, 57cr, 58c, 60tr, 60b, 61tr, 61c, 61b8b, 36c, 36b, 37cr, 38t, 38cl, 38cr, 38b, 39b, 41c, 43c, 44b, 47t, 47c, 47b, 50c, 55bl, 55br, 56tr, 56b; by courtesy of the National Portrait Gallery, London: 56c; Peter Newark's Pictures: 46c, 46b; Range Pictures: 14c, 29c, 31b, 33b, 39; British Library: 52c; Cadbury Ltd: 58b; Camerapix: 20b; A. Crichmay: 62tr; Darwin Museum: 39cl; Ford Motor Company Ltd: 59t, 59b; Hulton Deutsch Collection: 16b, 21t, 24c, 26t, 30c, 30b, 31c, 32c, 33t, 37b, 40b, 42c, 49cl, 50b, 54cl, 57b, 60tl; Image Select: 34t, 34c, 34b, 40cr; James Massey Stewart: 12c, 26b; Mansell Collection: 27b, 41t; Marks and Spencer plc: 63t, 63c; Mary Evans Picture Library: 6t, 8t, 9t, 12t, 13b, 15b, 21bl, 21br, 22t, 23t, 25c, 27t, 2t, 43t, 57cl, 58t, 59cl; still from the film Henry V by courtesy of the Rank Organisation plc: 54cr; Rex Features: 32t; Royal Geographical Society: 49t, 49cr, 49b (Lt. H.R. Bowers); Science Museum/Science & Society Picture Library: 37cl, 41b; Science Photo Library: 40cl, 42b, 51c; Theatre Museum: 62c; Tony Stone Images: 18b.

ILLUSTRATIONS
James Field: 10t, 10c, 11t, 11c, 12b, 17t, 17bl, 17br, 22c, 22b, 23c, 23b, 24t, 25t, 25b, 27c, 28c, 29t, 29cr, 29b, 51bl, 51br; David McAllister: 7t, 9c, 9b, 13c, 14t, 14b, 15c, 16b, 16c, 26c, 30t, 31t, 35t, 36t, 37t, 40t, 42t, 44t, 46t, 48t, 50t, 53t, 54t, 55t, 55c, 59cr, 61t; Bob Venables: 44cr.

t = top; c = centre; b = bottom; l = left; r = right